Wi......

# Dr. James W. Smith

Contributing Author:

## Dr. Langston D. Logan, Sr.
### Pastor of Lawson Chapel Baptist Church
### Roxboro, North Carolina

ISBN: 9781481112550

Scriptural References:  New International Version

# ABOUT THE AUTHOR

Rev. Dr. James W. Smith was born and reared in Franklin County, NC. He received his primary and secondary education from Perry's High School, Louisburg, NC and later attended North Carolina Central University where he received a Bachelor of Science Degree in Commerce and a Juris Doctorate from the North Carolina Central University Law School. He earned his Master of Divinity and Doctor of Ministry degrees from Andersonville Theological Seminary, Camilla, GA. He has done additional study at Southeastern Baptist Theological Seminary, Wake Forest, NC, Shaw Divinity School, Raleigh, NC and Ligoneer Valley Study Center, Stallstown, PA. Dr. Smith has served on numerous boards and committees in North Carolina.

He was an instructor at the former Durham Business College, Durham, NC and Kittrell College, Kittrell, NC. He served as Deputy Director, Wake County Opportunities, Inc., Raleigh, NC. Dr. Smith has over thirty-five years of legal experience; ten years as a practicing attorney in North Carolina. He was the founder and first President of the Vance County Black Leadership Caucus and served as the Northeast Campaign Coordinator for Congresswoman Eva Clayton during her first campaign for congress. Dr. Smith is an In-Prison Seminar Instructor. He has conducted seminars for Death Row inmates at Central Prison, Raleigh, NC and at the Federal Maximum Security Prison in Leavenworth, Kansas. He served as President of North Carolina Central University Law School Alumni, Secretary and Vice President, North Carolina Association of Black Lawyers, Vice Moderator at Large and Moderator of East Cedar Grove Baptist

Association, President of the Durham Interdenominational Ministerial Alliance of Durham and Vicinity.

In 1998, Dr. Smith was appointed to a four year term as Moderator of Moderators for the General Baptist State Convention of NC, Inc. Presently, he is a board member of the General Baptist State Convention, a member of the Board of Trustees, Apex School of Theology and serves on the Durham Steering Committee of the United Negro College Fund. He has served as Pastor of the Mount Calvary Baptist Church since March, 1991.

Dr. Smith is a North Carolina State Bar approved sponsor of continuing legal education, a trained mediator, church consultant, inspirational speaker and is constantly called upon to teach seminars on Church Conflict and Legal Awareness Issues. He is the author of the book, "Deal By Me."

# ACKNOWLEDGEMENT

One day I came home from work exhausted and frustrated. I was working for a law firm and also serving as the pastor of a church. I wanted to do ministry full-time but I also wanted to utilize my legal background in my ministry. I talked to my wife about my frustration and began discussing options with her. Finally she said to me, "Honey, as a pastor, you are fortunate and blessed to have a legal background, also. So why don't you use your legal background to help churches and pastors with church conflict and legal awareness issues? I thought it was a brilliant idea so I eventually asked the Dean of our Congress of Christian Education, East Cedar Grove Baptist Association to allow me to present a workshop at the next Congress of Christian Education Institute. It would be a workshop entitled "Church Law." For four nights we discussed legal issues that could affect churches and pastors. I was truly amazed at the excitement and enthusiasm generated by the workshop. From that workshop, I became aware that it was a ministry that I would enjoy presenting/conducting as well as the need for it among our churches and pastors. So, I want to give special acknowledgement to my wife, Barbara, who encouraged me to move in this direction and also supported me in the writing of this manual. I am very grateful to Dr. John D. Fuller, a former President of the General Baptist State Convention of NC, Inc. for having the confidence in me to perform the task of Moderator of Moderators for the sixty-two associations within our convention. It has been a delight to share with so many fine moderators. I also want to thank the pastors and moderators of the associations who have invited me to conduct workshops for them.

Thanks to the Mount Calvary Baptist Church family who supported me in all of my efforts as I attempted to serve the convention and the association. They tolerated my occasional absences and never complained even when I thought they had good reasons to do so. So to each member of Mount Calvary, I say, "thank you" and I will always be grateful to you for being such a caring and loving church.

To East Cedar Grove Baptist Association, I am grateful for your support. You elected me moderator to a four-year term; you gave me the opportunity to present my first workshop on Church Conflict and Legal Awareness Issues and you have constantly given me encouragement along the way.

There are many persons whose names I have not mentioned but who have been so instrumental in my becoming who I am.

# *DEDICATION*

This manual is dedicated to my mom, Mary A. Massenburg Battle, who nourished, loved, cared and supported me in everything I attempted to do. She was with me in my bad times as well as my good times; we shared so much together. Her strength and confidence in me helped me overcome some difficult moments in my life. She always told me, "Son, don't give up, you can make it if you try." Mom left me to be with the Lord on March 20, 1998. In her death, I am still learning from the things she taught me. "Mom, I love you."

# *INTRODUCTION*

When I was appointed by Dr. John D. Fuller, the President of the General Baptist State Convention of North Carolina, Inc., to a four-year term as Moderator of Moderators, one of the things the President stated at the time was that there were too many churches going to court, in court or coming out of court. Dr. Fuller was expressing a real concern of his and suggested that our council should work on the issue of church conflict.

I focused my attention on handling church conflict and legal awareness workshops for the Pastors and churches. It is a result of these workshops that I have concluded that a book or manual dealing with church conflict and legal awareness issues would be beneficial. This manual is not designed to discuss every issue that the Pastor/Church may encounter nor is it the author's intention to give legal advice.

It is not my desire to tell any Pastor or church what to do. I realized that in the Baptist Church, there is something known as "autonomy." Each church has the basic freedom to do as she wishes. I desire to raise the issues and you are free to take it for what it is worth. When I begin most of my workshops, I state in the beginning that my workshops would not be necessary if it were being held fifty years earlier, because our grandparents and great-grandparents would have thought it a penitentiary crime to take the church or each other to court. But now things are changing and we have no problems taking the church and each other to court. We will sue the church and each other now-a-days in a heartbeat. The theory now is to go for the deepest pocket. So why should I sue the pastor and deacons only, when I can sue pastor, deacons and church. That is now the prevailing attitude.

Hopefully, from the illustrations and personal references, you will find this manual both enjoyable and informative.

# TABLE OF CONTENTS

# *CHAPTER ONE*

## WHAT THE BIBLE SAYS

There are several scriptures that I wish to use in discussing church conflict and legal awareness issues. These scriptures are taken from The New International Version.

In the 12th chapter of Mark, verses 12-17, you will find these words. "Then they looked for a way to arrest him because they knew he had spoken the parable against them. But they were afraid of the crowd; so they left him and went away. Later they sent some of the Pharisees and Herodians to Jesus to catch him in his words. They came to him and said, Teacher, we know you are a man of integrity. You aren't swayed by men, because you pay no attention to who they are; but you teach the way of God in accordance with the truth. Is it right to pay taxes to Caesar or not? Should we pay or shouldn't we? But Jesus knew their hypocrisy. Why are you trying to trap me? he asked them, Give to Caesar what is Caesar's and to God what is God's. And they were amazed at him."

In the 13th chapter of Romans, verses 1-7, it says. "Everyone must submit himself to the governing authorities, for there is no authority except that which God has established. The authorities that exist have been established by God. Consequently, he who rebels against the authority is rebelling against what God has instituted, and those who do so will bring judgment on themselves. For rulers hold no terror for those who do right, but for those who do wrong. Do you want to be free from fear of the one in authority? Then do what is right and he will commend you. For he is God's servant to do you good.

But if you do wrong, be afraid, for he does not bear the sword for nothing. He is God's servant, an agent of wrath to bring punishment on the wrongdoer. Therefore, it is necessary to submit to the authorities, not only because of possible punishment but also because of conscience. This is also why you pay taxes, for the authorities are God's servants, who give their full time to governing. Give everyone what you owe him: If you owe taxes, pay taxes; if revenue, then revenue; if respect, then respect; if honor, then honor."

In the 6th chapter of 1 Corinthians, verses 1-4, you will find these words. "If any of you has a dispute with another, dare he take it before the ungodly for judgment instead of before the saints? Do you not know that the saints will judge the world? And if you are to judge the world, are you not competent to judge trivial cases? Do you not know that we will judge angels? How much more the things of this life! Therefore, if you have disputes about such matters, appoint as judges even men of little account in the church."

In Isaiah 1:18, it says "Come now, and let us reason together, says the Lord. Though your sins are like scarlet, they shall be as white as snow; though they are red as crimson, they shall be like wool.

Matthew 5:9 states, "Blessed are the peacemakers; for they shall be called the sons of God."

The Bible gives explicit directions as it relates to the church. In the text, Mark 12: 12-17 and Romans 13:1-7, Caesar represents the government. Those who would argue that the church has no dealing with the government may be surprised to know Jesus' response when he found himself in a tempting situation. In essence, the people wanted to know if they had to pay taxes on their money.

Jesus asked them to look at the penny to see whom it belonged. Once ascertaining that Caesar's inscription was on it, he told them to render unto Caesar the things that are Caesar's and to God the things that are God's. When we look at what Paul says in Romans 13:1-7, we realize that the government is of God and that we should not fear it. If we are obeying the laws, then there is nothing to fear. If the speed limit is 55 mph and we are traveling 55 mph, then there is nothing to fear or to be concerned about. The problem arises when we travel 85 mph in the 55 mph speed zone.

We do have the freedom to worship but not the freedom to do everything we want just because we are a religious institution. What would happen if one decides that he wants to go into the wilderness to construct a tent to worship wild animals? Perhaps nothing, unless there seem to be some great danger to the worshipper. But as soon as the worshipper decides that he wants to dig a well and put in some running water and a sewage system or get him a telephone and electricity, then he faces the possibility of having to deal with Caesar, the government.

There will be times when the Pastor and church will need legal advice and the assistance of a lawyer in preparing legal documents and dealing with many other issues of the church. The church, may at times, needs to have a title examination. At times the Pastor and the church may need to defend themselves. Do not attempt to do this on your own. Give Caesar his proper due.

However, there are matters that have no place in Caesar's court. That is, some matters should be dealt with among the congregation and not in court. 1 Corinthians 6 makes it very clear that as it relates to the church and members or members against each other, conflicts, disputes or other matters that may arise among them should be handled within the church body. Isaiah 1:18 and Matthew 5:9 emphase the importance of working and reasoning together.

These problems may be matters of doctrine, polity, constitutional or any other matters causing strife among church and members. Often, such conflicts cause permanent division among church membership; division such as a significant number of members departing from the church. Some begin new churches. It is believed that most Church Conflicts can be avoided. Most unresolved conflicts within the Baptist Church is a result of ignorance of Baptist Polity. Regardless of the Nature of the conflict, if the church adheres to Baptist Polity, in most situations the problem can be resolved.

# *CHAPTER TWO*

## CHURCHES DESERVE GOOD ADMINISTRATION

Good administration also means less conflict. A church is part of the cause which is just and right. It is the instrument of God. It is under the lordship of Christ. It is relating the gospel in all its fullness to all the needs of the people.

A church proclaims the good news and witnesses. This proclaiming and witnessing is not only within the walls of church buildings but beyond those walls wherever receptive people may be found. Leaders in this work of a church deserve the best guidance available, as do their co-workers and those who are the objects of their efforts. Much of this guidance can come from good administrative leadership.

### A church educates and nurtures.

A church is learning, teaching, educating, and nurturing. Happily, the emphasis of this work is maturing from the often-limited question "What?" to include the question "So what?" A church desires to help make some significant things happen. This is really the gist – the essence – of Christian education. It is the function of a church which deserves the best leadership a church can discover and develop. Good church administration can lead in the discovery and development of effective leaders in learning and nurturing.

A church ministers to persons in need. The number of persons in need continues to spiral. Their needs proliferate at a progressively faster rate. A church is a ministering organism. It attempts to minister unselfishly.

This attempt merits the best guidance a church can muster. Good administration can provide much of this guidance.

A church worships God; a church experiences His presence in an encounter which is life-changing and empowering. The members meet Him frequently and perhaps regularly in private and in corporate experience.

These encounters, in addition to providing benefits to the worshiping person as an end, also supply the stimulation, disposition, and spiritual power to enable the church to engage in all of its other work – proclaiming and witnessing, educating and nurturing, and ministering. Such encounters deserve to be multiplied and enhanced. Good church administration can help significantly in multiplying and enhancing the occasions of worshiping encounter.

Charles A. Tidwell states in his book, **Church Administration, Effective Leadership for Ministry,** the following: "The kind of leaders and leaderships a church needs and deserves rarely appears by accident. Leaders must use and know certain skills to be good leaders. It is imperative that the pastor offers no less than his best when the opportunity to lead comes to him. If one desires to pastor, there are some basic things he should learn. The church needs a good leader and leadership; the church deserves and requires both. God has promised His church His presence and His leadership, along with His power and other resources. Among the resources He has given are his people to lead."

There is tremendous information and opportunities for pastors and those who aspire to the ministry. Our churches deserve the best. "Can a blind man lead a blind man? Will they not both fall into a pit?" (Luke 6:39, NIV)

Once I was working with a church that was in the process of selecting a pastor. Finally, after an extensive search, they called a pastor. Well, sometime later I happened to talk with one of the deacons of the church and asked him how things were going. Interestingly enough he said to me, "Well, I don't know yet. We had our first conference meeting the other night and we found out that he did not know how to carry a motion."

I was a little complex, but it then dawned on me, "Why would you call someone who cannot carry a motion?" Hey, this to me was a true example of the "blind leading the blind." Most congregations are blind as it relates to the spiritual operation of the church. Therefore, the pastor of all people should possess a certain knowledge that garners the attention and respect of his flock. The pastor is the spiritual leader.

## Good administrators are good leaders.

Leaders move their followers and followers are moved by their leaders. Leaders make the difference, and training makes the difference in leaders. All leaders are born, but they are not born leaders. One might be born to a leadership position or come to the position by appointment, election or other power, including a divine call. But what is given or attained in any access to a leadership position is no more than an opportunity for one to become the leader for which the position calls. In today's society and more than ever, it is imperative that pastors be knowledgeable in their leadership position. Otherwise, we will continue to see the blind leading the blind.

The pastorate is a unique calling. It entails being a good administrator and leader. Within the congregation, there may be doctors, lawyers, engineers, teachers, electricians, scientists, etc. All of them may be experts in their field but when it comes to the spiritual work of the church, the pastor should be the expert in that field.

# CHAPTER THREE

## DOCTRINE – POLICY - POLITY

In the church and especially, the Baptist Church, conflict is inevitable. When problems arise in the Baptist Church concerning doctrine, policy or polity, they can lead to serious church conflicts. Often, such conflicts cause permanent division among church membership. I believe that most unresolved conflict within the Baptist Church is a result of ignorance of Baptist Doctrine, Policy or Polity. So, regardless of the nature of the conflict, if the church adheres to Baptist Doctrine, Policy or Polity, I believe the problems of conflict can be resolved.

Three words that are often confusing and used interchangeably in the Baptist Church are Doctrine, Policy, and Polity. I will give a distinction I feel may be helpful.

**Doctrine** is the teaching of the Baptist Church. It is more or less what Baptists believe by faith. Articles of Faith are generally found in the Baptist Hymn Book.

**Policy** is the rules, procedures and governance of the Baptist Church. In many Baptist Churches, this is spelled out in the Constitution and Bylaws of the church.

**Polity** is the form and character of the church; in other words, what makes one a Baptist Church. For example, can a church that does not baptize by emersion say she is a Baptist Church? Within the discussion of polity is when we hear most often the word "autonomy."

In the traditional Baptist Church, the power and authority is vested in the membership. This does not mean it is vested in a member. You know, the member whose grandparents donated the property where the church building sits or the member who gave the most to the church last year. This does not mean the member who is the child of some famous person of the church. I could go on and on but I am not talking about that kind of membership; I am talking about the collective body of the church. The power and authority are vested in this body. This body may be inclusive of the above.

Some time back, I received a letter from a pastor who had been dismissed from his pulpit. He was attempting to explain and answer some charges that had been levied against him by the deacons and congregation. He was making a very good case and I understood his position as he was responding to each charge. However, in one of the charges, the congregation accused him of not promoting and teaching the doctrine of the Baptist Church. In response to this charge, the pastors stated, "I do admit, I disagree with 'majority rule' by vote of the church conference in 'all matters' especially if the majority decision is plainly contrary to the Bible." He continued by saying, "Congregation rule is the Baptist policy but there is serious evidence that the New Testament Church led by the Apostles did not operate by this rule or standard."

Well, what do you say? I know that this position may very well have been the main reason for his dismissal.

In **Church Member's Handbook,** by Joe T. Odle, he states, "A Baptist church is simple in its organization. It is a self-governing body whose members have equal rights, privileges, and duties. It is probably the purest democracy the world has ever known."

I have a position that may be controversial to many and I have shared it in workshops. Here it is, "I believe if the Lord gives me a vision for the church and I share this vision with the church during our business session and the church does not vote to move in that direction, I should not get mad and upset with the church." At the very least, I should go back and pray that the Lord will give me directions and guidance and help me to present what He has given me in such a way that the congregation will be agreeable. This seems to be the only way. Short of this, we are embarking upon conflict.

# CHAPTER FOUR

## ETHICS, ETIQUETTE AND AUTONOMY

**Ethics,** Webster says is the discipline dealing with what is good and bad and with moral duty and obligation. It is a set of moral principles or values. In other words, it is literally knowing and doing what we think and know is right. Stephen Charles Mott, *Biblical Ethics and Social Change,* says that Christian ethics is a response to the grace of God that we have received in Jesus Christ. Mr. Mott asked the question, "What is the nature and content of our ethical response? "We love because God first loved us." John 4:19.

Often many churches get embroiled in conflict because they do not practice ethical behavior. Henry Ward Beecher says, "Hold yourself responsible for a higher standard than anyone else expects of you." As a church, when you do this you will be exercising standards required of the ministry. Here are a few simple principles for the Pastor that I believe can help.

1. Treat each member as though he/she is the most important one in the world, regardless of the station of the member or the tithes being paid.
2. Do not try to be all things to all people – learn to say no.
3. Practice honesty – unfortunately some folk believe there are degrees of this.
4. Do not leave everything for the last minute – be better prepared along the way.
5. Do not chase money. It will come. The Lord will provide.

Violating ethical principles can lead to serious conflict. For example, if someone misappropriates church funds, the church is headed for conflict. It is therefore important that certain checks and balances be put in place to readily ascertain if certain unethical or illegal matters are taking place regarding the church's finances. By doing so, the church is not expressing a distrust of anyone but rather operating as good stewards of the church's funds. Some things to be considered are internal audits and reconciliation of bank statements. If the offices of the financial officers are vacated for whatever reasons, then an outside audit should be considered. Often, when matters of misappropriated funds in a church occur, it is the pastor who is in the midst of the conflict even if he or she knew absolutely nothing about it. Therefore, it becomes imperative that the pastor implements safeguards to prevent as much as possible these occurrences.

Let's suppose the church's policy is for the treasurer and financial secretary to sign on all checks. Incidentally, the church policy should be that at least two people should sign on all checks. Assume that your financial secretary is busy, live some distance from the treasurer or will not be at church the following Sunday so he or she decides to sign a couple of checks for the convenience of the treasurer. This is bad business and should not be done. Remember that we are stewards of the church's funds and should treat it as such.

Another area of unethical conduct is Promiscuity. This behavior speaks for itself. One of Webster's definitions for promiscuous is, "not restricted to one sexual partner." In the Christian context, it is immoral and not becoming of a Christian. When a pastor becomes involved with a member of the church, it is potential conflict. Make no doubt about it. In one of my workshops, as this matter was being discussed, someone raised the question, "Dr.

Smith, I understand promiscuity as it relates to the pastor, but what about deacons or trustees." Well, the answer is that in all matters where this occurs in the church, it can lead to serious conflict.

We may also look at the area of disclosure as an unethical conduct. Failure to disclose has been a serious problem for a lot of ministers and especially those who may be candidates for a church. I hear the phrase said quite often, "If the Lord has forgiven me and has called me into the ministry, why do I have to share my past with anyone." Well, the simple answer to the statement is, you don't. The real question ought to be, "Do I want to be a successful pastor, or do I just want to get a church?" I have found from the workshops and calls that I get from churches and pastors that as long as things are going well at the church, no one is particularly concerned about the pastor's past. But as soon as something occurs that brings on opposition to the pastor, these same folks began digging into the pastor's background for negative information to use against him. Well, the pastor and or prospective pastor can minimize the impact of this by giving a full disclosure. Now, this does not mean that one has to give every little detail of some negatives in his or her background but one does need to inform or mention the matter or matters to the church.

As a former practicing attorney, I was primarily a defense lawyer. Well, one of the things I learned and used successfully in defending my clients was how to use my client's bad record. I found that it was much better for me to inquire of my client about his bad record and allow him to share it, than to ignore it and allow the prosecution to bring it out on cross examination. When I do it, the impact is minimized. If the prosecution does it, the impact is maximized.

I believe the basic concept works in the ministry. However, we must be realistic. Some churches are not going to be receptive, regardless. But what God has for you is for you. Some churches would not have called the Apostle Paul as their pastor. Once they reviewed his resume and observed that he had been imprisoned on occasions, he would have been finished. There would have been no attempt to find out the reasons or to get an explanation. Just the fact that it was mentioned was enough for him to be eliminated. Can you visualize what they would have missed, a man whose letters we read and preach on Sunday morning, a man who said, "For God I live and for God I die."

When I was being consider for the position of pastor at Mount Calvary Baptist Church, I had something in my background that I was not proud of and wished had not happened. I wished I could have relived the moments and done things differently but I realized that I could not. I knew that the Lord had forgiven me and I felt forgiven. But I realized that I needed to share it with the church.

Now I have no fear of anything that I may have done being exposed to my congregation and feeling some type of repercussion from it. I say to folks that if you were to share some negative information with my congregation, all they would say is, "Oh, I've already heard that, what's new."

At one of my workshops, I shared the following as I was discussing this issue. "If I were to share with you that the Lord called me in 1982 and I became ordained in 1986, then I do not have a problem with you checking me out from 1982 forward. Talk to members of my church. Talk to folks in the community where I live. Check me out. But don't go back to 1981. You may find something you don't like." If you must judge me, then look at me from my Damascus Road experience forward.

Here are a couple of things that the church can do to gain full disclosure.

1). Do a record check. This may include criminal and credit background.

2). Develop interview questions.

**Etiquette** is often confused with Ethics. There is a difference. Etiquette has more to do with conduct, procedure and how things are done. In this context, I like to refer to it as Ministerial Etiquette. How do you dress or carry yourself before the congregation or outside the church? Is my talk and language conducive to what I proclaim to be? What is my attire when I stand before the congregation to preach? What is your posture when you sit and stand? Do I perform the task I am given to do or do I take liberties to do as I please? This may sound humorous but actually "Etiquette" says a lot about you.

Here are a few tips that I believe will be helpful to the Pastor, Associate Minister and/or Assistant Pastor in the Baptist setting.

1. Associates and/or Assistant Pastors should not veer away from the Pastor's style.
2. Do not use or open your Bible while sitting in the pulpit. Stay attentive.
3. Do not preach before you preach.
4. Do not tell people to turn to someone else and tell them what to say.
5. If you are asked to do something by the Pastor, only do what you are told to do.

6. Be conscious of preaching time and prayer time. Most folk do not have long attention spans
7. Invocation is what it says – invoking the Lord's presence. This should not be long.
8. Do not ask people to use Bible at scripture time. It is to be read in their hearing.
9. If you are asked to have remarks by any Pastor, be very brief.
10. Do not preach after or before another person who is scheduled to preach.
11. Certain language may not be appropriate in the pulpit.
12. Do not fuss at congregation or air your dirty laundry from the pulpit.

Believe me, when folk develop a certain attitude, suspicion or dislike concerning you as a Pastor, conflict is more likely to occur.

**Autonomy** by definition is the right of self governing. The autonomy of the Baptist church clearly allows the majority vote of the church to determine policy. However, autonomy should neither overrule polity nor the Bible. If the majority of a church's membership rules against polity or the Bible, then it is my belief that the minority should have the right to appeal such ruling to its affiliate Association. Now, I realize that many churches are not affiliated with an association or convention. But this is my argument for affiliation. Every church should be accountable to someone else other than herself. Now the argument is, "We are accountable to God." When I hear that statement, to me, it is a statement to do as we please.

Many say they believe in autonomy but many don't practice it. Once I received a call from a minister who stated that he allowed a female to preach her initial sermon. Later the church voted to license her to preach. The minister's concern as expressed to me was that after his church had licensed the preacher, the association in which his church was affiliated, voted to exclude his church from fellowship and affiliation. The association did not recognize or license female preachers and no longer wanted to be associated with a church that licensed female preachers. The minister wanted to know what he and his church could do. This was an interesting situation to me. I thought that most churches and associations were licensing and ordaining females regardless of any personal belief. I later discovered I was wrong. Anyway, as I continue to ponder the matter, it occurred to me that this was truly an issue of autonomy. So let me poise these questions.

1) Does an association have the right to dictate to a pastor or church what it can or should not do? In my opinion, the answer is, no.

2) Can an association withdraw it fellowship and affiliation with a church because the church performs some act that is contrary to the belief of the association? In my opinion, the answer is, yes.

If we really thought through this from the issue of "autonomy," the only way this issue could be resolved is for either the church or the association to recognize the "autonomy" of the other. Therefore, since I believe in affiliation, the church should adhere to the practices of the association. However the alternative is for the associations to recognize the "autonomy" of its affiliated churches and not adopt rules and regulations that would encroach on the "autonomy" of the church.

Further considering "ethics – etiquette – autonomy," have you ever thought about how tradition and customs have evolved over the years in the Baptist Church? It has not been too many years ago when no one would consider standing when scripture is read. As a matter of fact, one would be looked upon strangely. Now-a-day, when scripture is read, those who sit seem to be looked upon strangely. Oh, I am not for or against either one. Personally, I believe in the freedom to worship as one pleases. If you are led to stand, then stand. If you are led to sit, then sit. Well, I am not raising this issue to be critical of standing or sitting when scripture is read but to highlight something that I think is important, "ethics – etiquette – autonomy." Think about this. A minister comes to your church and he is asked to read the scripture. He stands to read the scripture and says to your congregation, "Will you stand for the reading of God's word." Well, your congregation is not use to standing for scripture so his/her members stand and your members stay seated.

Or on the other hand, you attend another minister's church and you are asked to read scripture and because your members are not accustomed to standing for the reading of scripture, you announce, "Will you remain seated for the hearing of God's word." In both of these instances, some members are standing and some are sitting. Now, it may not be anything wrong with that but it just doesn't look good. "Autonomy" says that both of our churches have the right to stand or sit. But "autonomy" also demands that both churches respect the custom and tradition of the other. So would not it be better if both pastors would consult with each other regarding his/her custom or tradition before imposing his/her desire on your congregation. Now, that is true autonomy. Also, "ethics and etiquette" would require both to do the task they were asked to do.

# *CHAPTER FIVE*

## COMMUNICATION IN CONFLICT

### Communication is engaging in a civilized manner.

This is a major concern within the Baptist church and can cause major conflict. Congregations tend to find themselves at odds with each other over some of the most insignificant matters. As a result, a power struggle ensues and then the church finds herself in turmoil. One or both think they are correct in their position and neither wishes to refer to the other. A lack of understanding of Baptist Polity and a lack of Christian ethics only help to fuel the problems.

In addition to a lack of understanding of the Baptist polity and a lack of Christian ethics, I would like to suggest one simple word that I believe is key in our congregations. That word is COMMUNICATION. As I do workshops on Church Conflict, I am finding that congregations are having serious problems communicating with each other. Isaiah 1:18 says, "Come now, and let us reason together, saith the Lord: though your sins be as scarlet, they shall be as white as snow; though they be red like crimson, they shall be as wool." As Christians, we must find some way to discuss and communicate our concerns without allowing our emotions and anger to control us. During my years of service as pastor, I have learned that everyone is not going to agree with us on all matters even if we do say they came directly from the Lord. Frankly, I do not expect all my deacons or my members to agree with me all the time. I do expect that we will be civil enough to discuss and communicate with each other over our differences. "Come now, and let us reason together, saith the Lord." We must learn to communicate.

Let me share this with you. The pastor and deacons invited me to their church to mediate and help them in resolving their conflict. I went to the church and was greeted by one of the deacons who then led me into this beautiful conference room where there was a large elegant executive conference table. As I entered the room I noticed the pastor sitting in the high chair at the head of the table and the deacons sitting over in the corner. At first impression, it looked like a grasp for power. Let us look at this picture and suppose it had been the other way around. Suppose the deacons were sitting around the conference table and the pastor was sitting in the corner. Neither picture gave a good image. Anyway, I sat down and immediately ask the deacons to sit around the conference table. The pastor and deacons proceeded to tell me why they had invited me to come. I listened very attentively. When it was my time to speak, I attempted to relax everybody with what I call an ice breaker. There was a laugh or two but one could still feel the tension in the air. I continued by asking what I considered my most important question. I asked, "Brother Pastor, do you feel in your heart that we could possibly discuss and come to some resolution of this conflict?" The pastor looked me in the eyes and said, "Brother Moderator, I am going to be frank with you, the answer is, no." I then asked the deacons, "Brother Deacons, do you feel in your hearts that we could possibly discuss and come to some resolution of this conflict?" The deacons looked at me and said, "Brother Moderator, I am going to be frank with you, also. The answer is, no." Well, guess what I said and did. In case you can't, I looked them straight in the eyes and said,

"Now Brothers, why did you all invite me over in the first place?" After a few more words, I kindly said to them that I am not sure what I can do to help you and left.

Now let's think about it. Wasn't it shortsighted to invite someone over to help you resolve a conflict when you had no intentions of resolving it in the first place? Exercising humility and the ability to communicate would have gone a long way in helping to resolve this conflict.

## Communication is knowing how to be tactful.

Being tactful is exercising a keen sense of what to do or say in order to maintain good relations with others or avoid offense.

Some time ago, I had the pleasure of sitting in on a session for ministers. It was a very good session and everyone seemed to enjoy the session very much. One of our distinguish pastors taught the session and he talked about making changes in our churches. He used as his reference Dr. George McCaleb's book entitled, "Faithful Over A Few Things." I must admit that I was kind of tired as a result of the drive from Durham, NC to the session and I was having a hard time keeping my eyes opened. But when the distinguish pastor began talking about making changes in our churches, my eyes and ears opened because I knew that I had just heard something else to write about. Making changes in our churches- now that is a real conflict issue. You talk about combining the choirs, starting an eight o'clock services, dealing with the tenure of officers, changing the order of services, creating a new ministry, rearranging the flowers on the pulpit, and etc. Well, I have experienced churches splitting over changes far minor than the ones I have mentioned.

Now let me hasten to say that I agreed with the distinguish pastor. I believe changes are good for our churches. New ideas, new faces and new things can be very beneficial as we meet the challenge of ministering in this present age. I want to mention just a few things that was stated that I believe will help Pastors and churches to minimize conflict as changes are considered.

First, never change for the sake of change. There should be a purpose behind the change.

Second, it's not what we do; it is how we do it. Most of us can attest to the fact that any word or phrases used can be fighting words depending upon how they are used.

Third, learn how to maintain relationships. Again, being able to communicate and reason with each other is very important.

And so, as we look to fresh ideas and new ways of ministering to our congregations and at the same time consider church conflict, let us remember that being tactful is also good communication.

# CHAPTER SIX

## PASTOR AND DEACONS IN CONFLICT

A good relationship between Pastor and Deacons is essential if conflict is to be prevented.

The word for "Deacon" in the New Testament comes from the Greek word (Diakonos). This word means one thing, servant. Anyone who is a servant in the Greek language is a "Diakonos." In essence, when we consider the word "Deacon," we think of him/her as servants. We attempt to come up with all kinds of definition when talking about deacons. But the truth of the matter is, deacons are servants. I have often been asked to give the duties of the "Deacon." My brief answer is, "A deacon's job is to assist the Pastor, pure and simple.

In today's church, the Deacon's role has become more complex. He is to: (1) Assist in the preparation of the church's ordinances. (2) He is to visit the members under the leadership of the pastor. (3) He is to fill the pulpit when the church has no pastor. (4) He is to be the spiritual examples to the church. (5) He is the pastor's helpers and congregation's servant.

There are some things that the Baptist Church should note.

1. Deacons were not divinely appointed but their office rose out of need of the early church. In most of our Baptist Churches, deacons are ordained and it is through a process of what is called, "Laying on of Hands." This has given the perception that there is a "divine calling."

Deacons are not called by God, but are chosen by the congregation.

2.    There is no such person as a chairman of the board in the Bible, nor were there any deacon "boards" at all.    "Boards" have legal significance.    Pastors and Deacons are scriptural offices and denote spiritual and moral power and not legal power.  Now, let's not cause conflict in the church over what I just said.  If you have had deacon "boards" in your church for years and they are working find, let it be.  It's not a battle worth fighting.

3.    A deacon has no more power in the church than any other lay member.    In essence, deacons do not make the law and they are not the interpreters of the law.  The power and authority in the Baptist Church is vested in the membership.  Deacons do not give orders to the church but receive instructions from the church.  They do not make decisions for the church but carry out the church's decisions.

4.    Deacons are not the pastor's boss; his co-partner; nor are they equal to him in office or authority.  Deacons are to carry out the wishes of the pastor and church.  They are servants of the pastor and servants of the people.

Knowing all of this makes a good deacon.

Let us look at how power struggles developed in many churches.  Over the years, many rural churches were having services only once a month.  The Pastor was the Pastor of as many as four churches.  The Pastor found himself only at the church on Sunday mornings for worship services and at Bible study one day during the following week. Once every three month, the pastor went to the church for what was known as a conference (business) meeting. Generally this would occur on Saturdays and if the pastor lived some distance from the church, he would spend the night with a deacon or good member of the church. The only other times the pastor would find himself going back to the church would be in the case of death, an emergency or some other special occasion. This does not mean that the pastor was not concerned or was not busy. After all, he had four different churches in which he was responsible for as pastor.

Now, if we were to look at this picture, who do you think ran the church in the Pastor's absence? You guess right – the deacons. In most cases, it was the chairman of the deacons. So what makes one think that since he/she is now the full-time pastor, the deacon or deacons are going to readily give up this power and authority? In the deacons' mind, they know more about what is best for the church than you do. After all, they have been among the church folks all their lives and the pastor has just come on the scene. Would not it make sense to try to understand the deacons and began teaching Baptist polity, doctrines and love for one another rather than embarking on a collision course with each other.

With the best of intentions on everybody's part, some times conflict is unavoidable but as Christians we are admonished through scripture to do our best to resolve it among ourselves.

J. Alfred Smith in his book, *Deacons' Upholding the Pastors' Arms,* states, "In many Baptist churches, pastors are not clear about the role deacons should play. This lack of clarity has been the basis for the tension and conflict which sometimes exist between pastors and deacons. At pastors' conferences the problems of pastor-deacon relations are discussed in formal and informal sessions. Many pastors who have had unfavorable experiences are fearful of deacons and seek to control the conflict by limiting the authority of deacons and there are deacons who seek to control the conflict by limiting the authority of pastors." Only when the Pastor and Deacon truly understand his or her role and learn to communicate with each other will conflict be resolved.

Pastors attempting to change the tradition of the church can also cause much conflict. Originally, the conflict seems to be with deacons who, in their perspective, try to protect the church. This is a rather difficult matter to discuss. But it is necessary because much conflict occur over this in the Baptist Church, in particular.

As a moderator, I had the occasion to attend a number of Installation Services for Pastors. On a number of these occasions, I have heard the minister who was making the charge to the pastor state words to this effect. "Now, remember that you have been called as the pastor of a Baptist Church." I believe that what the minister was saying is that there are some things that Baptists practice, which are a part of the tradition of the Baptist church and these practices may be different than other churches or denominations.

It would be very difficult to change the mode of baptism in the Baptist Church from immersion to sprinkling. Likewise, it would be difficult to say the church will only participate in Holy Communion twice a year. Maybe it does not have anything to do with salvation but Baptists believe that baptism should be by immersion and that the church should take of the bread and cup often.

At least more than twice a year, for as often as the church does it, she does it in remembrance of Him. In the same way that the church holds to her doctrinal beliefs, she also has very strong feeling about certain of her traditions. Baptists do not practice washing feet every Sunday. Baptists do not practice the teaching of the speaking in tongues. Baptists understand that the Bible speaks of these things. Jesus washed his disciples' feet. The disciples washed each other's feet. Many folk in the Bible spoke in tongues. On the day of Pentecost, they spoke in other tongues. It is not the belief, but what Baptist regularly practices. So, if a pastor of a Baptist Church is being led of the Lord to go in a different direction, that is, to wash feet every Sunday, to teach the speaking in tongues, to lay on hands and anoint with oil at every prayer, etc., this may become a source of serious conflict.

Just as it seems I am running out of things to say something interesting comes to my ear. I was sitting down watching the television, a book in my hand and sleep on my mind when the telephone rang. When I answered, the voice on the other side said, "Dr. Smith, we have been reading your articles and we just need to talk with you." "Well, I have no problem talking if you want to come this way because my schedule won't allow me to come that way anytime soon," I said. Well, a group of individuals made that trip to Durham and boy was it an interesting discussion.

The sad thing about this discussion was that these individuals expressed a love, dedication and loyalty for their church but they were among the minority in their support of their Pastor. Now before I continue with this, let me first say that some of my best colleagues are in denominations other than Baptist. As a matter of fact, I have had the opportunity to preach for them and many have preached for me. So this article is not about denominations but about the Baptist Church.

Well, let me share with you some of the conversation. These members expressed to me that they had been members of the church for many years and really wanted the best for the church but they felt helpless. I asked, "What do you mean by being helpless?" "Dr. Smith, we are just seeing our church move completely away from a Baptist Church," they said. I then became very interested in what they were about to say since I had heard that kind of talk coming from many congregations. So they continued by telling me that they had selected a Pastor who had been with them for about two years or less and when he first came things seemed to be going just fine but then things changed. Well, I took that to be sour grapes since I have come to realize that most congregations have problems accepting change. But the more I listened, the more I became intrigued by their conversation. "Tell me what's going on," I said. They spilled their guts. "Dr. Smith, he anoints with oil and slay folks every Sunday. He doesn't invite any Baptists to preach for any occasions at the church. He has removed all officers and silences members who opposed what he does. His whole emphasis is on the younger members and he has forgotten about the elderly. At conferences, he will not recognize anyone whom he knows or feels is in opposition to him. He even stated from the pulpit that we should pull out of the General Baptist State Convention and stop sending our money and use that money here in the community. Dr. Smith, he's just got the chairman of the deacons in his pocket because he supports everything he does. Our church is now broke and he seems to want all the money for himself. He has a majority of the members, who are younger, supporting him because they like the excitement." They finally closed by saying to me that they were not use to that kind of church because their previous Pastor had been with them over thirty years and was a great supporter of the convention and was a traditional Baptist.

Obviously, I was a good sounding board for them and understood some of their concerns. However, I was unable to help them solve their problems.

# CHAPTER SEVEN

## INTERIM PASTOR AND ASSOCIATE MINISTERS

Another area of potential conflict within the church has been that of "Interim Pastor" and Associate Ministers." A congregation asked me to help it with language to insert in bylaws regarding the Pulpit Committee. They were discussing the "Call" and the "Termination" of a Pastor. In the midst of this, a question was raised, "Dr. Smith, what is the best way to fill the pulpit during the interim while you are in the process of selecting a pastor?"

Well, I said, "Churches use a number of ways, some call different ministers each Sunday, some use their associate ministers, and some have what they call, Pastor of the month, etc." I gave a couple of ways in which I had seen churches do this. However, I stated to them that I believed the best way to fill the pulpit during this time was with the use of an interim pastor, preferably one who had retired and who would be willing to work with the church until a selection was made. I stated to them that they would want to make sure the church had an agreement with the interim pastor expressing that he would not be interested or a candidate for the church. Now many of my comrades don't agree with me on this issue that the interim pastor should not be a candidate for the church. They feel that the interim ought to be able to express his/her interest for the vacant position.

Well, expressing my preference to the congregation opened a can of worms. They had already witnessed a couple of churches that were using an interim pastor, in turmoil.

Well, what happens is this. An interim pastor comes in, he begins preaching like he/she never preached before, visiting the sick, bringing new members into the church, cultivating a good relationship and doing all the right things. Invariably some members of the church and especially those who became members under the interim pastor, fall in love with him/her and believe that he/she should become the Pastor. Well the old guard remembers the agreement and what the interim pastor had said. And they also began to see the interim's personality change, a little too much of this or that for them, so they want the committee to continue its search for a pastor. Now here comes the interesting part. I discussed this with some of my brothers in the ministry and they have said to me, "Well if a majority of the church wants him, the church is autonomous; they can do what they want to do." Well, I agreed. The Baptist Church is autonomous and she can do mostly what she wants to do. But when a minister accepts the church as an interim and signs an agreement to do certain things, then he has a responsibility to uphold his end of the bargain. Ministers have an obligation to serve with integrity and with the highest degree of moral ethics and if the congregations can not expect that from ministers then no wonder they fight among themselves.

It is interesting that the word "interim" is defined as "an intervening time." What I have been able to observe from my experience is that the shorter the intervening time, the less conflict occurs. Interims should realize that their job is not to set the church in order but to maintain stability until a pastor is called. A good "Interim Pastor" wants to see a pastor called as soon as possible.

    1) Interim Pastors are not interested in ordaining deacons and ministers.

2) Interim Pastors are not interested in fostering buildings programs.
3) Interim Pastors should not be interested in placing their friends are relatives into the pastoral position.

All of this do nothing but cause further conflict.

Every once in a while, some minister, church member or even an Associate Minister will engage me regarding the duties or functions of an Associate Minister. Questions are asked such as, what is the difference between an Associate Minister and an Assistant Pastor? What is an Associate Minister's duty and what is his/her relationship to the Pastor? Does an Associate Minister have any authority and rights in the Church? How often should the Pastor allow the Associate to preach? A member will even ask on occasions, "When is the Associate Minister going to preach?"

Congregations need to be educated and instructed that it is the Pastor's duty and responsibility to shepherd the flock. It is the Pastor's scriptural obligation to preach, teach and care for the flock. Now, the Pastor may ask someone else on occasions to help in this area. For some Pastors, Associate Ministers are a pest. For some Pastors, Associate Ministers are a blessing. It depends upon ones perspective and how he/she sees the role of the Associate Minister. Now let me emphasize that I would hope that all Pastors would see the Associate Minister as a blessing since we are all in this ministry together and working towards one goal. This discussion should not be taken negative or as an indictment of Associate Ministers. As matter of fact, all Pastors at one time or another have perhaps been an Associate Minister.

First, there is a difference between an Associate Minister and an Assistant Pastor.

Associate Ministers are generally members of the Church or who have associated themselves with the church. It is not an appointed or elected office of the church. An Associate Minister has no more authority and rights in the church than any other member. Having said this, the Associate Minister should recognize that the "call" itself bestows upon him/her everything that's needed.

Assistant Pastors may or may not have been members of the church or associated with the church when called to the ministry and the position may be classified as an office. In many churches, the Assistant Pastor may be a paid position.

More importantly both serve at the pleasure of the Pastor to assist him/her by performing certain duties specified by the Pastor in keeping with the Word of God.

I was asked to come and share with a church on the process of selecting a Pulpit Committee. We talked about how the Pulpit Committee should be diverse to include all elements of the church. Others felt that it should only consist of deacons and trustees. Interestingly, the church had a number of Associate Ministers and it seemed that many of them were asserting themselves in the position of the Pastor. Some of them thought that by virtue of their being the Associates, they should automatically take charge of the services until a Pastor was called. Of course, we dealt with all of these issues and the church selected a diverse Pulpit Committee. However, when the meeting was over, one of the deacons shared with me that he told the Associate Ministers that once they accepted the called, they gave up any rights to assert any authority or power in the Church. I thought that was rather harsh, but when I thought about it, the deacon may be right. Their authority and rights are no more than any other member of the church.

# *CHAPTER EIGHT*

## TRUSTEES AND FINANCE OFFICERS

The Role of Trustees has legal significance. It also has the potential to cause conflict within the church if the role is not properly defined. Because the Role of Trustees has legal and business significance, many churches have mistakenly chosen persons with comparable backgrounds and relying less on spirituality. I think this can be a big mistake when choosing trustees in the church. If there is anyone who should be a Christian, it should be the trustee. Remember that the trustee function has legal and business significance.

The work of trustee in a church will vary according to the structure within which the church operates. In most instances they will be the official group to sign papers and otherwise represent the church in legal matters. They thus will act as the agent of the church in transacting business. In some cases the pastor acts as the agent of the church. It is important that the pastor or the trustees know and have evidence of the authority possessed in acting for the church. If a pastor or trustee enters into a contract outside that authority given them by the church, it could result in personal liability for any loss or damage to the church or any outside party. When acting for the church, there must be clear indication of the role of agent on behalf of the church. This will eliminate any personal liability in the case of a dispute. Advice from an attorney can be helpful in this area.

In some organizational structures, trustees may perform additional responsibilities for the church. They may act as the Building and Grounds or Maintenance Committee, the Personnel Committee, or serve in functional areas relating to insurance and like matters. However, it is important that they function in a professional, ethical and Christian manner. It is important for trustees to understand that they do not make the decisions for the church. They may recommend and suggest matters they feel will help improve the church. Their primary function is not to make decisions but to carry out decisions and directives of the church. Because of the nature of the Role of Trustee, sometimes trustees take on a 'power mentality.' They forget that the power and authority in the Baptist Church is vested in the membership.

Let me give just a brief example of something for you to consider. Let's suppose that the church votes to do a project for the church so long as it does not exceed Fifteen Thousand Dollars ($15,000.00). The trustees and or pastor if he is acting as agent decides that they know what is best for the church and enter into a contract to purchase a little more expensive material which ends up costing Twenty-Five Thousand Dollars ($25,000.00). If the church decides not to ratify the actions of the trustees or pastor, they may be personally liable for the balance over what the church voted on. Just something for you to think about, as this can really cause conflict.

# CHAPTER NINE

## SELECTING AND TERMINATING PASTORS

Selecting and terminating a pastor can be an interesting scenario. The termination of a pastor seems to cause more conflict than the selection of a pastor. However, I have been a witness to both instances.

One Sunday, I was at the church when the phone rang. It was the deacon of a church in an adjoining county. He asked me if I would be available to mediate a situation within the church. The church had a constitution and bylaws committee that stated that the perspective pastor must receive at least a two-thirds vote of the membership. As I considered this policy, it looked and sounded good on the surface. I believe that any pastor would want to be elected by at least a two-thirds majority. However, in this church, there were a few folks who opposed the composition of the pulpit committee. Every name that was brought to the church by the committee, they would vote in opposition, therefore depriving the church of the necessary votes by as many as five or six votes. I agreed to go to the church for the purpose of talking with the deacons, trustees and pulpit committee. As a result of this meeting, I was invited back to meet with the total church membership. It was an interesting meeting as the dialogue showed some very intriguing dynamics. One thing surfaced and that was the opposition felt that the pulpit committee did not have diverse representation. To show their displeasure, the opposition took each opportunity to vote against the candidate regardless of his or her qualifications. Once we discussed the importance of getting a pastor, allowing the opposition to express their feelings and creating an atmosphere where a genuine discussion of issues could take place, the congregation very shortly thereafter elected a pastor. The thing to remember is that one never really knows what the problem or conflict may be until a line of communication is opened. Sometimes it can be very helpful to bring resource persons into the church to assist with matters of this nature. Congregations are very curious folks. They may or may not talk among themselves, but they will talk to someone else.

Terminating a pastor can create a lot of strong emotions. In most instances the pastor has developed a rapport with many members and invariably there are some who want him to stay and others want him to go. The very strong emotions show when it is a divided house. Working through this conflict within a church can be a very difficult process.

Consider this factual situation with me. The pastor was interested in having the church approve some guidelines or policies he had developed. He brought the matter before the deacons to be discussed but the deacons did not like the policies for whatever reasons and refused to support and recommend them to the church body. Well, the pastor decided to take the matter directly to the church. In presenting the matter to the church, he intimated that if the church did not approve the policies he would resign. The pastor was actually trying to get approved policies and guidelines that would give him, he thought, authority to replace officers who had been in a certain position for what seemed like an eternity along with other things he felt would be in the best interest of the church. Well, the church failed to approve the policies and guidelines and the pastor offered his resignation to become effective ninety days forward. The church at that meeting voted to accept the resignation. Somewhere in between the time of his offering the resignation and its effective date, the pastor obviously began thinking about whether he had made the right decision. So, he decided to abbreviate his list of demands and took them back to the church at a regular business meeting and stated words to this effect. "If you all accept these guidelines, I will consider staying." The church discussed the abbreviated ones and voted to accept the guidelines by a slim majority. Lo and behold, the Sunday after the ninetieth day, the pastor was back in the pulpit to the dismay and anger of many members.

Obviously, the church began to be in turmoil. The pastor and deacons called me in to help resolve the situation to no avail. However, from the discussion, the pastor's position was that once he told the church he would consider staying if the church approved the policies, and the church then approved the policy, they were also voting to rescind his resignation and to reinstate him as pastor. The opposition felt that once his resignation was accepted, he was obligated to leave the pastorate and the only way he could remain as pastor would be for him to follow the same process as any other prospective pastor by applying for the position.

Now, I admit that I am not so sure which position is the right one. However, I do know that the source of the conflict in this matter rests with the pastor. Can't you see through this? The pastor attempted to call the hand of the church and he failed. The message here in this conflict situation is for pastors to be careful what we say when trying to prevail.

If, for whatever reason, a pastor decides to resign his position as pastor, the prevailing rule among the Baptist

Church, in the absence of any documents, is that he shall give a written notice to the church stating the same. His notice of resignation shall be ninety days prior to the date of his departure. The church, however, may accept an earlier departure date. All salary and benefits cease on the departure date of the pastor unless specified differently by the church or contractual agreement between the pastor and the church. If the pastor's effective termination is immediate, the church shall compensate him in a lump sum equal to three months benefits.

Another issue raised during discussions of this matter is funds being held by the Pastor's Aid Committee. The Pastor's Aid Committee has accumulated a sizable sum of money and members want to know whether the money belongs to the church or the Pastor. The prevailing rule is that the Pastor's Aid Committee exists for the benefit of the Pastor. Any funds held in the committee become the funds of the pastor once he is terminated. Please note that this is the prevailing rule in the absence of a contract or policy to the contrary.

I would like to share this with you. I was asked to assist a church that had been taken to court by the Pastor who had "resigned" or as he said "forced out." It was the Pastor's position that he was forced out and the church owed him for three months' salary. Of course, the church's position was that he left on his own and that the church was not obligated to compensate him for three months' salary.

This case was moving through the legal system after having been filed a couple of years previous. It had now reached the point where the Pastor and the church were required to participate in mediation. I was contacted to assist the church in this mediation process. Legal fees in this matter for just one of the parties at the stage of mediation, had already exceeded $10,000.00. As in most church matters, the judge did not want to hear the case. The courts would prefer that these matters be settled prior to court.

I am sharing this because as I sat there watching the former Pastor and this church negotiate back and forth over what amount the Pastor is entitled to received, it created an eerie feeling in my spirit. The money that was spent for legal fees, court costs, mediation fees, etc. could have very well gone for ministry. It could have gone to State Missions, Shaw University, Central Children Home, Lott Carey, etc. It certainly made me reflect.

The point that I make to Pastors and churches is that in matters of conflict, it would best serve all parties to seek a way to solve the issues without resorting to court action.

# CHAPTER TEN

## TO INCORPORATE OR NOT INCORPORATE

In most states, a church is not required to incorporate as a nonprofit religious corporation. However, the effect of incorporation is to create a legal entity that the law recognizes for purposes of holding title to real estate, executing contracts and performing all functions necessary in conducting the civil affairs of the church. It does not take away the spiritual nature or purpose of the church. For example, assume your church owns and operates a church van and someone is injured as a result of the church's negligence or assume someone slips and falls as a result of your church's negligence, and you are sued. If the church is not incorporated, legally each member has potential liability. On the other hand, if the church is incorporated, then only the church, herself, is exposed.

In discussing this matter with pastors and churches who have been interested in the advantages and disadvantages of incorporation, many have asked, "Well, won't our insurance take care of that if we are not incorporated?" "You know, if our church is found to be liable and we have a one million dollar policy," obviously, in most situations, the answer is yes. But the church needs to make sure she has sufficient coverage; otherwise, a member or members may still be exposed to any liability in excess of the one million dollar policy. It is always good to discuss these matters with a local attorney who is knowledgeable of the laws affecting your state.

Often these questions come up, "Do I need to get a 501 (c)(3) for my church?" "Is my church considered a non-profit if I don't have the tax exempt status 501 (c)(3)?" Well, I advise pastors and churches to seek legal advice for matters they have specific concerns because what's good for one church may not be the same for the next church. From my perspective; however, I don't believe in getting a tax exempt status 501 (c)(3) for the church. Many churches that are involved in Day Care Centers, Housing, Senior Citizens Ministries, Grants, etc. should have a tax exempt status 501 (c)(3) but I would create another entity for that purpose. For example, I would incorporate XYZ Baptist Church Foundation and then acquire the tax exempt status 501 (c)(3) for that particular entity.

Many Pastors and church members have called me to request a sample copy of bylaws. While I do not object to providing them with a copy, I do want to emphasize that taking one set of bylaws and adopting them as your own can create serious problems for your church and lead to obvious conflict.

Now there are some things that should be basically the same. Let's take the "Preamble" for example. Every Baptist Church should declare and establish their constitution and bylaws to preserve and secure the principles of their faith and to govern the body in an orderly manner. The "Preamble" should have language that will preserve the liberties of each individual church member and the freedom of action of the body to other churches. The autonomy of the Baptist Church demands language of this nature or something similar. In addition, it helps to put all of our Baptist Churches on the same page.

Consider the "Purpose" and the "Statement of Basis Beliefs" of the Baptist Church and one should conclude that this should be basic language for our churches. The purpose of our church should be to give visible form to that faith and fellowship to which God has called His people. We should acknowledge ourselves to be a local manifestation of the universal church through which Jesus Christ continues to minister to the world by His Holy Spirit. We should seek to fulfill this calling through corporate worship services, through a program of Christian nurture by which the membership may be strengthened in their faith and love through the proclamation of the Gospel of Jesus Christ by word and deed, and through ministering to human need in the name of Jesus Christ. Likewise, we should affirm the Holy Bible as the inspired word of God and the basis for our beliefs. We should voluntarily band ourselves together as a body of baptized believers in Jesus Christ personally committed to sharing the good news of salvation of lost humankind. The admission of members and the termination of members should be basically the same for all of our churches.

# CHAPTER ELEVEN

## CONSTITUTION AND BYLAWS

We use these words interchangeably, but actually there is a difference in the "Constitution" and "Bylaws." However, most churches labeled them "Constitution and Bylaws." The Constitution is more of polity. Polity is the character of the church; in other words, what makes the Baptist church a Baptist Church. Generally this is spelled out in the PREAMBLE, STATEMENT OF BASIC BELIEFS AND CHURCH COVENANT.

The Bylaws are rules adopted by the church chiefly for the governance of its members and the regulation of the affairs. This can and may vary depending upon the church. Generally, bylaws would include discussion about Church Membership, New Member Orientation, Rights of Membership, Church Officers Responsibilities, Auxiliaries and Committees, Church Ministries, Church Ordinances, Special Church Meeting, Provision for Handling Grievances, Quorum, Operational Manual and Amendments. Any other matters that the church deem important for discussions or the promulgation of rules, should go in the bylaws.

I found that in my workshops, talking about "Church Incorporating" and "Constitution and Bylaws" were the touchiest issues to discuss with Pastors and churches. So, I make it my point to say that your church is autonomous and you can do what you want.

Often, a clergy friend and I engage in conversations related to the church. And whenever I mention "Constitution and Bylaws," he will say to me quickly, "I am not having them in my church. If it can't be solved with the Bible, it won't be solved, because the Bible has the answer to all this conflict." As quickly as he could make the statement, I agreed with him that the Bible has all the answers to our conflict. What I try to get the church to see and understand is, the "Constitution and Bylaws" is primarily for Ceasar, the government, and not necessarily for the church. I have had a Constitution and Bylaws at the church I pastor for years, and I have only referred to them on a couple of occasions; such as, how many do we need for a quorum, etc.? As a former attorney, I have shared with pastors and churches that of all my years being in and out of the courthouses when church matters were before the court, I have never seen or heard the presiding judge ask the attorneys representing the parties in the church dispute, what does the Bible say about that? But I have seen and heard them ask, what does your Constitution and Bylaws say about that particular issue?

On a number of occasions, I have been asked by pastors and lay persons whether or not a church should have a constitution and bylaws. Some have expressed to me the position that it makes the church too legalistic. Others have stated that they don't need any document in their church that dictate to them how to run the church and that the Bible is their sole authority. Then there are those who believe that the church should have a constitution and bylaws because it gives some order and direction for the church. Well, I could go on and on with the pros and cons of this question. However, I wish to stay within the context of church conflict and in doing so I want to highlight my concern.

Prior to beginning a legal awareness workshop I was doing for a church, I stated to the membership that forty or fifty years ago a workshop of this nature perhaps would not be necessary because our grandparents would have thought it a penitentiary crime for the church or members to take each other to court. Unfortunately, however, today that is not the case. In every county within this state, if one would check the court records, I would venture to say that there is a least one church that is in litigation over some church conflict issue. We air our dirty laundry in spite of what the Bible says in 1 Corinthians 6, "Dare any of you, having a matter against another, go to law before the unjust, and not before the saints?" Well, having said this, I believe the constitution and bylaws can be a very helpful document for a church and would ask you to look at this actual factual situation in arriving at a solution for your church.

A church within our convention was having some serious internal problems. Some of their problems involved the pastor and some of the problems related to the deacons/trustees relationship. It eventually got so bad that one of the trustees filed an action with the court. In his action, he asked that the pastor and certain of the deacons be enjoined from coming to the church or at least from meddling in the church business affairs. Prior to deciding the merits of this case, the judge appointed me to mediate the matter with the hope of settling the dispute within the church. I was given the expressed authority to counsel the church members, certify the membership, bring the matter to a vote, and report the findings to the court. As you may suppose, counseling fell on deaf ears and I was left with certifying the membership and having the church vote on the matter. Well, what's interesting about this is that members on both sides begin to share with me about who ought to be voting. Some stated that they had sisters and brothers who were members that were living up north and they wanted to send them ballots. Others felt they didn't need ballots and that everyone should be present and cast his/her vote by standing. Then there was the age thing and whether or not some members were too young to vote because they did not understand the issues involved. Would all members or just active members vote and if only active members voted, then what constitutes an active member? I am certain that there are many more questions that the reader of this column would have.

Well to bring some closure to this, I would suggest that if you are a pastor or a church that believes all persons who have put their names on the membership roll should be eligible to vote regardless of the issue involved; then you may not need a constitution and bylaws. However, if you believe that some clarity and directions should be given regarding your membership; then you may want to consider having a constitution and bylaws for your church. Fortunately for me, this church had bylaws that gave some directions in this matter. It would have been very interesting to see how I would have proceeded without anything to guide me in this situation.

Let me interject that your constitution and bylaws will deal with many more matters than just membership but this situation is only to help you consider the issue as you arrive at a solution for your church.

It is important to remember that "one size does not fit all." There are some things that are unique only to your church. Whether you have five or twenty-five persons on your Pulpit Selection Committee and whether they are all deacons or a representation of the church body is a matter for your church to decide. Whether women will serve as deacons or how many persons will be needed to constitute a quorum is a church matter. So please do not adopt sample bylaws as your own without first adjusting them to fit your situation. You see, my bylaws may call for a business/conference meeting once every three months and you may want one every month, depending upon how much you like to argue. "Just kidding".

# CHAPTER TWELVE

## RECOGNIZING LIABILITY AND OTHER LEGAL ISSUES

Bruce P. Powers, in his book, *Church Administration Handbook,* says that one of the most difficult areas with which the church must relate is that of the law and the legal ramifications of the church and its feelings of immunity or separation from the state. Many churches act out of ignorance or a stance based on the separation idea, which says that the church has no dealings with the state. Every church will have need for legal advice at some point in its ministry. The need will vary according to the kinds of activities, building programs, and ministries in which the church is involved. A major consideration in this area will involve the ability to know when to seek legal help and the best approach to take when the situation calls for it.

**The issue of "liability"** is taken for granted by many churches. Churches feel that if they have sufficient insurance, liability is something they don't have to worry about. Churches and minister are not immune from responsibility for their action because they are in the religion business. Often, most "liability" issues arise from the negligence of the church or member. Negligence is basically the failure to do or not do what a prudent person would or would not do under ordinary circumstances. Many churches leave themselves vulnerable to lawsuits because of negligent acts.

Let's assume for illustrative purposes that the church owns a couple of vans. On any given day, the van is being used to transport individuals to Sunday School, church services, Bible Study, etc. Suppose the driver of the van is speeding and as a result an accident occurs. The church may be exposed to liability. This happened to a church in my association. Individuals were injured as a result of an accident involving the church van and the church was sued.

I was doing a workshop at a church once, and someone asked this question, "Dr. Smith, if someone comes out of the baptismal pool and slips and fall, injuring himself, is the church liable?" I responded by saying this, "There is a saying in law that every dog has one bite." I proceeded by sharing this story. "You are walking down the block in your neighborhood and you see this same little dog in the neighbor's yard. He has never in the past barked or attempted to bite you. However, on this particular day, he slips up behind you and snags you on the leg. You get very upset, mad and decide to bring a lawsuit against the owner of the dog. Well, chances are you will not prevail under the theory that every dog is entitled to one bite. On the other hand, let's assume that a month after your incident, another individual is walking down this same block in the neighborhood and this same dog slips up behind him and snags him on the leg. If the individual can show that the dog had bitten someone else in the past, then he would perhaps prevail in a lawsuit against the owner of the dog based on the dog already having had one bite.

I shared this with the individual who asked the question to point out that in that particular matter, the church would perhaps not be liable. However, now that the church is aware that the area around the baptismal pool is slippery, it is the church responsibility to remedy that situation. When I am doing workshops for trustees, I give lots of illustrations so that they can appreciate and understand the need to remedy negligence by the church. Think about your playground. Do you have signs up that say, "caution, play at your own risk." Think about the caretaker who cleans the church. What precautions are being taken to make sure no one injures himself in a slip and fall. It may be wise to put a sign out while you are cleaning that says, "caution," floor wet." Are you having services immediately after a big snow or ice storm and you know that the steps have not been cleaned, salted or de-iced? Trustees, especially, should make sure that safety is a priority. We never think about it in these terms, but anytime monies are expended for anything other than ministry, the upkeep and building of the kingdom, we are not being good stewards.

**Privilege Communication and Employment Practices** are matters that may result in "liability" to the church. Pastors and deacons, specifically, need to treat the matter of Privilege Communication very seriously. The relationship between Pastor and Pew is a confidential one and should never be breached. In other words, whatever the parishioner shares with the Pastor in confidence must stay confidential. Counseling for Pastors can sometimes be a tricky business; therefore, it is always wise to know your limits. As Pastors, there may be some things you are not equipped to counsel about. For example, a parishioner who has suicidal or homicidal thoughts my need more than just spiritual counseling.

I had been doing workshops for awhile before I realized or thought about Employment Practices as being an issue of "liability." But at one of my sessions, someone raised the question, "Can the church get sued for employment discrimination?" Immediately it hit me. Bruce P. Powers, *Church Administration Handbook,* says, "A church would do well to establish a procedure for dealing with disputes, disagreement, or grievances that are bound to develop in spite of the best of Christian intentions. It is tragic when such disputes make it to the court system to be resolved." The way the church handles employment practices could prevent the church from a discrimination lawsuit. To illustrate this, let's suppose two musicians apply for the position of Minister of Music at your church. One of these individuals is very musically talented and gifted but does not attend church on a regular basis. He or she does not possess the Christian attributes. The other individual is an average musician, attends church on regular basis and possesses the Christian attributes. With this information, most churches would employ the individual who is an average musician, attends church on regular basis and possess the Christian attributes. Once the average musician secures the job, the talented and gifted musician files a lawsuit alleging employment discrimination. These are just a few issues that the church needs to be concerned with to be protected from "liability" issues. One of the ways to handle a situation of this nature is to develop a job description. The "job description" can create the criteria the church thinks is pertinent to the position.

There are a number of issues that our churches are dealing with on a regular basis. I wish to raise these issues for the benefit of our churches. Many times we are not conscience of these issues and often proceed with business as usual until we run into trouble.

1. When was the last time your church had a fire drill and does the church have large exit signs displayed? (On this issue, the church may want

to check with the fire department or public safety to ascertain what the church needs to do.)

2.     Are caution and warning signs posted at the church in places where members and the general public may be exposed to a present danger? (It is very important to inform members and the general public of places and matters that may be of danger to them. Failure to do so could subject the church to liability.)

3.     Are staff members and employees of the church performing their duties in ways that will not constitute negligence? (The church needs to know that failure of staff or employees to do something that should be done or doing something that should not be done may constitute negligence. If an employee or staff member of the church is deemed to be negligent; then, his/her action may be imputed to the church and such negligence may result in the church being liable, financially. A legal workshop involving dos and don'ts of the staff and employees may be helpful to the church.)

4.     Is the pastor aware of his/her professional, ministerial and ethical responsibilities and duties to his/her parishioners? (The pastorate is just like a doctor/patient or a lawyer/client relationship. It is a pastor/pew relationship. Please be aware that whatever is told to the pastor in confidence must go with him/her to the grave; unless, permission is given to divulge the information. There are many instances where improper counseling or bad advice has resulted in the pastor and church being liable. The pastor

needs to know when matters are beyond his/her capabilities. Making referrals when necessary is always good.)

5. Does the church have any guidelines or personnel policy in place to deal with personnel matters? (It would be helpful for the church to have something in place that would speak to personnel problems. A procedure for handling grievances is always helpful.)

6. Is the church incorporated? (There are no requirements in North Carolina for a church to be incorporated; however, it may be wise to get some legal advice on the advantages and/or disadvantages of incorporation. Regarding issues of liability, the church and membership may be affected.)

7. Does the church keep good financial and tax records? (If the church is issuing checks for the payment of services rendered as an employee or independent contractor, you need to ascertain the tax obligations and responsibilities.)

These are just a few issues that may have legal consequences for the pastor and church. It is my hope and desire that you consider them.

**Keeping good financial record** and treating taxes with a lackadaisical attitude are shortcomings in many of the Baptist Churches. It is important to keep good financial records. The financial records should include up-to-date income and expense statement and balance sheet. And these records should be detailed. The church should keep a record of the members giving and be prepared to share with any member when requested, his financial giving. I tend to argue this point very forcefully because often we treat the finances as if it is our money. But in actuality, it is God's money and we are only stewards of His money. In other words, His money is in our trust and the care of "trust money" not only has legal consequences but spiritual consequences as well.

It is also a function of the church to make sure that the taxes are properly paid. Don't believe it, churches do get audited. I have talked and shared this statement with many pastors who don't take this matter seriously and they will say to me, "The Internal Revenue Service is not interested in my little church." How shortsighted this statement is. The audit trail of a member may very well lead to your church. Failure to keep and report proper deductions may lead to an audit. The fact of the matter is, the Internal Revenue Service has no respecter of person when it comes to taxes.

I often illustrate the above point by stating that I grew up in a very rural area of North Carolina. There were very few residents living in the community and they often lived miles apart. So, most of us never stopped at stop signs because we very seldom saw vehicles approaching. We would just slow down and keep getting up. When I got my driver's license at the age of sixteen, I began doing what everybody else was doing. And I did it for years until on one occasion, the highway patrol was approaching and I received a ticket for failing to stop at a stop sign. What I say to my comrades who say that churches don't get audited is, "You may go for a long time but it doesn't mean you won't get stopped."

As a side note to pastors, let me say that it is difficult to drive and own a vehicle or vehicles costing in excess of $100,000.00 with a reported salary of less than

$50,000.00 and not expect to be targeted by the Internal Revenue Service.

As I travel doing workshops, I am constantly observing churches. Many of these churches have very beautiful structures and are implementing great ministries. In essence, finance does not seem to be a concern for these churches. Now, I realize that when it comes to finances in the church, most of us think in term of our tithes and offerings. But many churches are also considering other means of support for the church.

**Living after death** is an issue I want to focus on of which I think we need to concern ourselves. I am talking about our funding a ministry, a church library, an education building, etc. in our name. I call this living after death. Think about this. What's wrong with continuing after death our stewardship to the church we confess to loving and caring about during our lifetime? Why not think about a life insurance policy leaving the church as beneficiary. Let's talk about this in terms of Wills and Estates.

In *Church Administration Handbook* by Bruce Powers, he says, "The whole matter of wills and estates represents a significant area of legal concern for the church and the Christian interested in the total concept of stewardship. The advice of those trained in the field is essential for good planning because of the complex nature of government rules and state laws regulating the disposition of an estate. Many churches have a special committee to promote the concept of making a will or establishing a trust as an act of Christian stewardship. Some churches are fortunate enough to have attorneys, bankers, or accountants who can assist church members in this area."

The advantage of estate planning and the need to put things in order should be evident to the Christian. The desire to protect one's assets in the way an estate is settled should be of major concern. Good planning will minimize the effect of taxes and other administrative costs relating to settling the estate. It also provides for the effect of taxes and other administrative costs relating to settling the estate. Finally, it provides for the efficient and timely distribution of property.

If we are to consider living after death, then the making of a will is essential to the completion of estate planning. Without a will, state laws specify who benefits from the estate. By making a will, we can specify who is to benefit. The complexity of legal terminology is such that we may not say what needs to be said unless an attorney assists with the preparation of the will. We should be encouraged to make a will so that those of us who have supported the church while living can continue that support in the disposition of the assets of our estate.

# CHAPTER THIRTEEN

## RESOLVING CHURCH CONFLICT

Resolving conflict in the Baptist Church is never easy. Brian Schwertley, "Conflict Resolution in the Church," says that professing Christians desire peace in the body of Christ. Many acknowledge that peace and purity can only be maintained through biblical church discipline. Brian Schwertley argues that Matthew 18 is a crucial passage for preserving the peace and discord of believers, because in it, Christ sets forth the steps necessary for dealing with sin between believers.

Here are some pointers for resolving church conflicts. The core of this process can be stated simply:

(1)     identify the issue, the area of concern or conflict;

(2)     clarify the goals or wants of the various parties;

(3)     search for alternatives that enable all parties to achieve as many of their goals as possible; and

(4)     covenant to follow the chosen alternative.

Every person has basic innate needs. The activity of one's life seeks to fulfill this set of needs. In order to fulfill these needs, a person works towards goals. Goals are things that do not now exist but that we can imagine existing. In other words, goals are targets towards which we direct our actions. We are intentional, goal directed beings, seeking the fulfillment of our needs through the achievement of our goals, and we are beings who must pursue our goals in social settings. Thus, we have the clash because many are trying to occupy the same space at the same time.

"Resolving Conflict" means helping others be "edified." "Resolving Conflict" means striving for effective communication. "Resolving Conflict" means identifying goals and the primary issue. "Resolving Conflict" means developing alternatives for goal achievement.

Try hard never to allow conflict to spread to the point of consuming the energies of the whole church. Practice the followings:

** Never allow the growth of the church to shift emphasis away from the value of the individual.

** Hold leadership retreats for spiritual and relational development.

** Promptly respond to complaints. Things seldom right themselves.

** Reject a wait-and-see attitude

** Acknowledge there's a problem and call for prayer and fasting.

** Hold spiritual life meetings with a neutral visiting speaker.

** Exercise church discipline when appropriate.

** Involve neutral mediator to settle the disturbance.

** Prayerfully determine if there's an evil core to the conflict, and start church discipline

** Balance grace and justice

Developing a "Church Conflict Resolution Policy" can be very helpful. The purpose of the policy is to provide for the staff and members of the church with a formal procedure for the resolution of problems or conflict arising in a fair and orderly fashion if such problems cannot be resolved informally. In simple terms, it would be a process that all members would be required to participate administratively in exhausting their remedies before proceeding to court. Some churches have dealt with this with language in their Constitution and Bylaws; such as, "Neither this church nor member(s) of this church shall bring an action against another member without exhausting his/her remedies through procedures adopted by this church before bringing any action in a court of law." To make sure that members are parties to the adopted procedures, it may be worthwhile having members to sign upon receipt of same. Here again, contacting an attorney to discuss this matter could be very helpful.

It is worth noting again that a process of resolving conflict by mediation within the church is as follows:

1) It is done voluntarily
2) It takes place in an informal setting
3) It uses a neutral third party
4) It gives decision making power to the disputants

The two most common forms of resolving church conflict are mediation and arbitration. Mediation assists the disputants in collaborating on a solution; only disputants decide on the solution. Arbitration is the process whereby the dispute is resolved by an arbitrator who listens to both sides and then renders a solution. In some situations, parties can appeal the solution; in other, they cannot.

In resolving conflict or grievances, Bruce Powers, says that a written procedure should include the following ideas.

1. The immediate supervisor should be the first person involved when an employee has a problem.

2. A written record should be made of the grievance and the attempt to deal with it.

"Several efforts may have to be made to resolve the issue. If the difficulty cannot be dealt with at the initial level, then the next level of supervision should be involved.

If the supervisors cannot develop a satisfactory solution, it is helpful to have some type of a committee (personnel, pastor/church relations) made up of qualified church members who relate to personnel matters. These persons would be brought into the discussion to give greater insight into possible solutions." Mr. Powers says.

You can't avoid conflict forever, but you can choose how you will handle it.

# CHAPTER FOURTEEN

## REASONS TO COME TOGETHER

### The church is too important.

As Christians, being a part of a church where there is little or no conflict is very comforting. Although conflict is inevitable, coming together to resolve it is the Christian thing to do.

Matthew 16:13-19 states that when Jesus came to the region of Caesarea Philippi, he asked his disciples, "Who do people say the Son of Man is?" Their reply was that some say John the Baptist; others say Elijah; and still others, Jeremiah or one of the prophets. "But what about you?" Jesus asked. 'Who do you say I am?'

Simon Peter answered by saying, "You are the Christ, the Son of the living God."

Jesus replied, "Blessed are you Simon, Son of Jonah, for this was not revealed to you by man, but by my Father in heaven. And I tell you that you are Peter, and on this rock I will build my church, and the gates of Hades will not overcome it. I will give you the keys of the kingdom of heaven; whatever you bind on earth will be bound in heaven, and whatever you loose on earth will be loosed in heaven."

The King James Version says, "The gates of Hell shall not prevail..." It is my belief that unresolved conflict is nothing but hell in the church. Realizing that the church is not ours but Christ's, should cause us to do whatever is in our power to resolve the conflict.

### Thinking and talking things through is always helpful.

No one has all the answers. Learning to listen and be willing to hear another viewpoint is always helpful.

Remember that each church member is equally important and there is value in everyone. Always keep in mind that the purpose is to resolve or solve the problem. One can never lose focus of the reason for coming together.

In Rick Warren's book, *The Purpose Driven Church,* he states, "In Nehemiah's story of rebuilding the wall around Jerusalem, we learn that halfway through the project the people got discouraged and wanted to give up. Like many churches, they lost their sense of purpose and, as a result, became overwhelmed with fatigue, frustration, and fear. Nehemiah rallied the people back to work by reorganizing the project and recasting the vision. He reminded them of the importance of their work and reassured them that God would help them fulfill his purpose." Remember the purpose for coming together and be reminded to pray and ask for direction and guidance as you engage in resolving the conflict.

### It gives cooler heads a chance to prevail.

It also gives a chance to cool heads. Proverbs 15 gives great insight to what happens when we proceed with great caution and discipline. "A gentle answer turns away wrath, but a harsh word stirs up anger. The tongue of the wise commends knowledge but the mouth of the fool gushes folly. The tongue that brings healing is a tree of life, but a deceitful tongue crushes the spirit." Proverbs 15:1, 2 &3.

It is very hard to resolve conflict when everyone is headstrong, upset or even angry with each other. Coming together gives everyone an opportunity to sit back and cool off. In every situation or almost every situation, there is generally someone who is reasonable. And coming together gives "reason" a chance to speak.

**It helps to bring about trust.**

There is nothing better in a conflict situation than to see trust develop among each other; a trust where each other rely on the truthfulness or accuracy of each other. They believe each other. No one is trying to get the upper hand but everyone acting in good faith. This is also best achieved when we accept the value of each other. We may not agree on every issue but we accept that you have the right to your opinion. Now let's see what we can do to resolve our differences.

**It helps the church to reflect.**

Oftentimes, churches split because they do not reflect on what they have already accomplished or wish to accomplish. Members are too engrossed in their own right or wrong positions until they do not see the big picture.

Philippians 3:12-14 says, "Not that I have already obtained all this, or have already been made perfect, but I press on to take hold of that for which Christ Jesus took hold of me. Brothers, I do not consider myself yet to have taken hold of it. But one thing I do: Forgetting what is behind and straining toward what is ahead, I press on toward the goal to win the prize for which God has called me heavenward in Christ Jesus."

I am reminded of a story that I heard from a minister who was campaigning for the position of President of the National Baptist Convention. He stated that he went to this church and when he arrived he saw a big sign in the yard that read, *"The main thing is to keep the main thing the main thing."* As he entered to go inside the church, he saw the same slogan above the door. He went to the pastor's study and he saw the same sign on the door entering the pastor's study, *"The main thing is to keep the main thing the main thing."* He said that when they went into the sanctuary, hanging up in front of his eyes was the same slogan, *"The main thing is to keep the main thing the main thing."*

The main point made here is to stay focused. Always reflect on who you are and whose you are.

# CHAPTER FIFTEEN

## SUGGESTIONS AND SAMPLE DOCUMENTS

### Suggestions for Pulpit Search Committee

1. Pray, Pray, Pray
2. Announce a vacancy in your church through your local association, state convention, etc., indicating what you are looking for in a pastor.
3. Receive resumes.
4. Write a letter informing applicants that you received his/her resume and will be in contact with him/her as soon as feasible.
5. Review resumes.
6. Put aside those resumes that do not fit what the church is looking for in a pastor.
7. Write a letter thanking the applicant for applying but tactfully sharing that his/her experience is not suitable for the church's needs at this time.
8. Keep the ones you think are possibilities.
9. Review resumes again narrowing them down to three or four.
10. Once narrowed down to three or four, make plans to visit their church during a worship service, if they are pastors. Let the applicant know you are coming. Do not sit together. Do not stand as a visitor. Do not hang around afterwards.
11. Check references.
12. Of the three or four, narrow them to two and invite each of them to preach and teach at least twice at the church.
13. Listen to comments of the congregations.

14. Ask questions like, do you attend Sunday School, evening worship, prayer meeting, Associational meetings, state and national convention. (This helps you to learn of his/her pastoral philosophy.)
15. Tell him/her what the church financial package will be.
16. After praying and the church believes that God is leading the church towards one of these applicants, recommend the number one (1) choice. Try not to present two names.
17. Ask the Chair of Deacons to call a Church meeting where the Pulpit Committee can recommend the applicant.
18. If the membership selects him/her, inform the applicant in writing by sending it by overnight express. Tell him/her of percentage of votes and the financial package you are offering.
19. Give him/her a date to accept or reject the call.
20. Inform the other two or three applicants of the church selecting another person. Thank the applicants for their interest in the pastoral position.
21. When the applicant accepts the call as pastor, the Pulpit Committee should resign.

## Suggestions for Pulpit Committee Interview Questions

1. What do you feel your role as a full-time pastor of the church would  be?
2. Do you feel that the church is a place for politics? Why?
3. Are there any reasons in which you would not marry a couple?
4. How important do you feel that being punctual and prepared for all services are?
5. Would you continue and support programs/events that have already been implemented in the church?
6. What vision do you have that will enhance the continuing growth of the church?
7. Which one do you believe is more important preaching or teaching?  Explain.
8. Would you accept another engagement, if known that service is going on at the church?
9. What is your opinion of females holding leadership roles?
10. What is your opinion of auxiliaries having anniversaries?
11. What is your opinion of fundraisers?
12. How would you reach and relate to all age groups?
13. Do you feel that the church is an important instrument in the community?  Why?
14. How important are community and civic government in your role as pastor?
15. What method do you have for getting to know your members?
16. How do you feel about confidentiality between pastor and member?

17. What is your position on the "Full Gospel, Tongues, Prophesying, Healing, etc?

18. Have you any experience with church building, renovation projects, developing music programs, etc.?

19. Do you feel the pastor should be involved with finances of the church? If yes, how much involved?

20. What would you consider to be or anticipate being the most challenging aspect that you will face as a new pastor?

## Suggestions for an orderly conference (business) meeting

1. The purpose of Hiscox/parliamentary Procedures
   A. It is to allow for an orderly discussion of issues in a deliberative body.
   B. Without some orderly discussion of issues, it would be impossible for the body to function.
2. Who is responsible for chairing the meeting
   A. Moderator/Pastor
   B. A designee of Moderator/Pastor
3. To maintain parliamentary courtesies, a member is expected to:
   A. Stand when addressing the Chair, as in making a motion, discussing a question before the body, etc.
   B. Sit down promptly when finished talking
   C. Do not speak during the business session except when addressing the Chair and then only after having been properly recognized
   D. Never talk or whisper to another member during the meeting.
   E. Confine discussion to the question before the body
4. The responsibility of the body
   A. Should be willing to accept decision of the majority
   B. Should be punctual for meetings
5. Discuss the business process and motions

## CONSTITUTION AND BY-LAWS
## OF
## XYZ BAPTIST CHURCH

### PREAMBLE

We declare and establish this constitution and by-laws to preserve and secure the principles of our faith and to govern the body in an orderly manner. This constitution and by-laws will preserve the liberties of each individual church member and the freedom of action of this body to other churches.

### ARTICLE I
### NAME

This body shall be known as XYZ Baptist Church worshipping in _____ State of _____.

### ARTICLE II
### PURPOSE

The purpose of this congregation is to give visible form to that faith and fellowship to which God has called His people. We acknowledge ourselves to be a local manifestation of the universal church through which Jesus Christ continues to minister to the world by His Holy Spirit. We seek to fulfill this calling through corporate worship services, through a program of Christian nurture by which our membership may be strengthened in their faith and love through the proclamation of the Gospel of Jesus Christ by word and deed, and through ministering to human need in the name of Jesus Christ.

## ARTICLE III
## STATEMENT OF BASIC BELIEFS

We affirm the Holy Bible as the inspired word of God and the basis for our beliefs. We accept the Scriptures of the Holy Bible as the inspired record of God's revelatory actions in human history and the authoritative basis for its doctrine and practice. We voluntarily band ourselves together as a body of baptized believers in Jesus Christ personally committed to sharing the good news of salvation of lost humankind.

## ARTICLES 1V
## CHURCH COVENANT

We adopt the following covenant as a means by which our members may express their intent to accept the lordship of Jesus Christ in the affairs of daily life. This document shall be subject to review and revision by the congregation as new insights from the word of God shall indicate ways in which our faith and life may be brought into closer accord with the teachings of the Scriptures.

## CHURCH COVENANT

(You may want to share the Church Covenant here)

## ARTICLE V
## POLITY
## SECTION 1:

The government of this church is vested in the members who compose it. This church is subject to the control of no other ecclesiastical body, but it recognizes and sustains the obligations of mutual counsel and cooperation which are common among Baptist churches. None of the Boards, Committees or Auxiliaries of this church can usurp the church's executive governmental or policy-making powers.

## SECTION 2:

(Include the church's affiliations)

This church shall maintain affiliation and cooperation with any other conventions, as the majority membership shall desire.

## ARTICLE VI
## CHURCH MEMBERSHIP
## SECTION 1: ADMISSION OF MEMBERS

This is a sovereign and democratic Baptist church under the lordship of Jesus Christ. The membership retains unto itself the exclusive right of self-government in all phases of the spiritual and temporal life of this church. The membership reserves the exclusive right to determine who shall be members of (Name Church) and the conditions of such membership.

## SECTION 2: CANDIDACY

Any person may offer himself or herself as a candidate for membership. All such candidates shall be presented to the church for membership in any of the following ways:

(1) By Baptism — A person who confesses Jesus Christ as Lord and Saviour and adopts substantially the views of faith and principles of (Name Church) and is baptized by immersion may be received into the fellowship of this church.

(2) By Letter — A person who is in substantial accord with the views of faith and the principles of this church may be received by letter from any other Christian church.

(3) By Christian Experience — A person of worthy character who has formerly been a member of a Christian church who is in substantial accord with the views of faith

and principles of this church may be received upon a statement of their Christian experience.

(4) By Watchcare — A person who is a member of another Christian church but living in this community for a brief period of time may be received into the membership of the church.

(5) By Restoration — A person who has lost membership may be restored to membership upon the recommendation of the Membership Committee and a vote of the church.

## SECTION 3: RIGHTS OF MEMBERS

All members on the active church roll is entitled to vote on all issues submitted to the church in conference, provided the member is present, except for the following:

(a) On all legal matters such as land purchase, borrowing money, building or renovation of church facilities and constitutional amendments, a member must be eighteen (18) years or older.

(b) For the call or dismissal of a pastor, a member must be eighteen (18) years of age or older.

(c) No member of (Name Church) shall bring a legal action against the church nor shall the church bring a legal action against any member without first exhausting his/her administrative remedy. For this purpose, administrative remedy shall include: (Name administrative process for resolving conflict)

## SECTION 4: TERMINATION OF MEMBERSHIP

Membership in (Name Church) shall be terminated by the following ways: (1) death of the member; (2) dismissal to another church; or (3) exclusion by action of the church. No names shall be removed from the membership roll of the church except by a vote of the congregation.

## SECTION 5: DISCIPLINE

It shall be the practice of (Name Church) to emphasize to her members that every reasonable measure will be taken to assist any troubled member. The pastor, other members of the church staff and deacons are available for counsel and guidance. The attitude of members toward one another shall be guided by a concern for redemption rather than punishment.

Should any member become an offense to the church and its good name by reason of immoral or unchristian conduct, consistent breach of his/her covenant vows or by willful refusal to be governed by the directives of the church adopted by the members, the pastor and deacons shall take reasonable measure to resolve the problem in accordance with Matthew 18, Galatians 6 and First Thessalonians 5:13-24. If it becomes necessary for the church to take action to exclude a member, a two-thirds vote of the members present is required. This action shall be taken ONLY after faithful efforts have been made to bring such a member to repentance and amendment. All such proceedings shall be pervaded by a spirit of Christian kindness and forbearance.

The church may restore to membership any person previously excluded, upon request of the excluded person, and by vote of the church upon evidence of the excluded person's repentance and reformation.

## ARTICLE VII
## PASTOR
## SECTION 1: GENERAL RESPONSIBILITIES

The pastor is responsible for leading the church to function as a New Testament church. The pastor shall lead the congregation, the auxiliaries and the church staff in the performance of their duties. The pastor shall preach the gospel, administer the ordinances, watch over the membership, have charge of the spiritual welfare of the congregation and the stated services of public worship. The pastor shall be an ex-officio member of all boards, committees and auxiliaries of the church. The pastor shall be the Moderator and shall preside at all business meetings of the church and church council except when good taste dictates otherwise. In accordance with acceptable Baptist Polity, the Pastor shall be the sole person to call meetings of the church body. In the event the Pastor refuses to call a meeting after being requested to do so, a majority of Deacons or a petition signed by at least fifteen (15) percent of the active membership may proceed to call a meeting of the congregation upon giving notice at least two consecutive Sundays prior to said meeting.

**SECTION 2: PULPIT COMMITFEE**

When it is necessary to call a pastor, the church shall select a representative pulpit committee consisting of not less than _____ but no more than _____ members. It shall be the duty of this committee to take necessary steps to secure a pastor. The committee shall investigate the merits of every candidate under consideration in regards to personal character, education, ministerial record and general fitness for the pastorate of this church. The committee shall recommend to the church only one name at a time to be accepted or rejected.

**SECTION 3: CALL OF A PASTOR**

The call of a pastor shall come before the church at a meeting of the congregation, notice of such meeting and its purpose having been printed in the bulletin and announced at least two (2) Sundays prior to the meeting. Election shall be by written ballot, with an affirmative vote of two-thirds (2/3) of the members present and qualified to vote necessary to extend a call provided there be present a quorum of at least twenty (20%) percent of the active membership.

## SECTION 4: TENURE AND COMPENSATION

The pastor shall be called for an indefinite period of time. The salary and compensation shall be fixed at the time of the call and shall be reviewed annually prior to the preparation of the church budget. The following factors shall be considered in implementing salary increases: (1) increases in collections over the previous year; (2) increases in members over the previous year; (3) overall financial condition of the church; and (4) effectiveness of the church's program. All salary increases shall be effective January 1 of each year. The Minister Salary Guidelines shall be used as a guide in determining the pastor's salary.

## SECTION 5: TERMINATION

The pastor's term of office may be ended upon ninety (90) days of notification on the part of the pastor or the church by mutual consent. Should the church decide to terminate the services of a pastor, a vote of the congregation shall be taken at a call meeting; notice of such meeting and purpose having been printed in the bulletin and announced at least two (2) Sundays prior to the meeting. A vote of a majority of the members present and qualified to vote, provided there be present a quorum of at least fifteen (15) percent of the active membership, shall make a valid termination. A pastor who is terminated by the church for reasons other than gross misconduct shall receive at least three months compensation and benefits. The termination shall be immediate and the compensation shall be rendered in not more than thirty days.

## SECTION 6: ASSISTANT PASTORS

In the event the church considers it wise to have one or more assistant pastors, the pastor shall be given the authority to select such assistant(s) subject to consent and approval of the active membership.

## ARTICLE VIII
## CHURCH OFFICERS

(Name the elected offices)

## SECTION 1: PASTOR

The duties of the pastor are set forth in Article VII, Section 1.

## SECTION 2: CLERK

The clerk shall keep a complete record of the transactions of all business meetings of the church. This record shall be read for approval at the next business meeting. The clerk shall preserve on file all communications and written reports and give appropriate notice of all meetings where such is required by the Constitution and By-laws. The clerk shall prepare all resolutions issued in the name of the church. The clerk shall maintain an up-to-date roll of the membership of the church. The clerk shall make available all records and documents of the church in his or her possession when authorized by the church. The clerk shall deliver immediately to his or her successor all books and records for which he or she has been responsible as clerk. All official documents and records of the church shall remain at the church in such facility as provided by the church.

## SECTION 3: TREASURER

The treasurer shall have custody of the funds of the church and all the deposits made in the name of the church. All checks drawn by the treasurer shall be in the name of the church. The treasurer shall receive all monies given in the name of the church or its auxiliaries other than those so designated by the church. Within twenty-four (24) hours of receipt, the treasurer shall deposit in the appropriate bank account all monies given in the name of the church. The treasurer shall insure that deposit bags are retrieved from the bank. The treasurer shall be bonded in an amount set forth by the church.

## SECTION 4: FINANCIAL SECRETARY

The financial secretary shall furnish members of the church envelopes for contributions to the church. He/She shall maintain an accurate accounting of all contributions given by members and annually distribute personal statements to all members listing their gifts. The financial secretary shall keep an accurate account of all monies received by the church and prepare a weekly statement for the treasurer and pastor. The financial secretary shall prepare regularly reports detailing all receipts and disbursements. The financial secretary shall prepare and present at the first church meeting of each year a cumulative report indicating the balance of accounts from the previous year, the total receipts and disbursements from the recent year and the beginning balances for the current year. The financial secretary shall be bonded in an amount set forth by the church. All church business and financial matters relating to boards and auxiliaries should be kept at the church.

## SECTION 5: (Name other offices)

# ARTICLE IX
# CHURCH COUNCIL

The church council shall be responsible for prioritizing church matters relating to financial expenditures and to assist the pastor in preparing the church calendar.

The church council shall consist of the pastor, presidents or representatives of auxiliaries, and chairpersons or representatives of boards.

# ARTICLE X
# BOARDS/MINISTRIES
## SECTION 1: DEACONS

The church, in conjunction with the pastor, shall elect deacons who shall be ordained to their work according to Acts 6:1-8 and 1 Timothy 3:8-13. In accordance with the meaning of the word and the practice of the in the New Testament, the deacons are to be the servants of the church. Their task is to serve with the pastor and church staff in performing the pastoral ministries tasks of (1) leading the church in the achievement of its mission; (2) proclaiming gospel to believers and unbelievers, and (3) caring for the church's members and other persons in the community.

As the need arises, this office may be filled upon recommendation from the pastor and deacons to the church to be considered by the church at a meeting of the membership. Persons recommended to the deaconship must pass the test of moral qualifications as listed in Acts 6:1-8 and 1 Timothy 3:8-13. Gender references shall not be interpreted to preclude women serving as deacons.

Deacons shall serve as council of advice and conference with the pastor in all matters pertaining to the welfare and work of the church. With the pastor, deacons are to consider and formulate plans for the constant effort and progress of the church in all things pertaining to the saving of souls, the development of Christians and the extension and growth of the Kingdom of God.

By proper organization and method among themselves, they shall establish and maintain personal fraternal relations with, and inspire oversight of, all the membership of the church. Especially are they to seek to know the physical needs and the moral and spiritual struggles of the membership and to serve the whole church in relieving, encouraging and developing all who are in any such need.

In counsel with the pastor and by such methods as the Holy Spirit may direct in accordance with the New Testament teachings, deacons shall have the oversight of the discipline of the church. In administering discipline, they shall always be guided by principles set forth in 1 Thessalonians 5: 12-24, Matthew 18 and Galatians 6. The deacons shall be free to call upon any member of the church to aid in discipline.

In case of illness or inability of the pastor, subject to advice and conference with him when possible, the deacons shall serve as a Pulpit Supply Committee. In any period when the church is without a pastor, unless the church shall otherwise provide, the deacons will arrange for temporary ministry and take counsel with reference to securing a pastor. It is not intended in any way to prejudge herein the method by which the Pulpit Committee shall proceed in securing a pastor.

**SECTION 2: DEACONESSES**

The deaconesses shall assist the pastor in developing the spiritual life of the women and girls of the church for the best possible Christian service. They shall cooperate with the pastor and the deacons in visitation, the care of the sick, the needy and distressed members and in the preparation of the observances of the ordinances of the church.

## SECTION 3: TRUSTEES

The church shall elect trustees consisting of not less than _____ and not more than _____. Persons who serve as trustee should meet the following qualifications: (1) be a person of the Word; (2) possess spiritual sensitivity; (3) be a team player, and (4) have skills in property management and upkeep and financial matters. The chairperson of the Deacons shall serve as ex-officio members.

The Trustees shall meet on a monthly basis with special meetings as the need arises; provided, that there be a quorum of fifty (50) percent plus one of the elected officers. The trustees shall hold in trust all property belonging to the church and shall take all necessary measures for its protection, management and upkeep. It shall have no authority to buy, mortgage, lease or transfer any property without a specific vote of the church authorizing such action. It shall designate the bank(s) where the funds of the church shall be deposited. The trustees shall secure and supervise the work of a custodian at such salary as authorized by the church.

The trustees may organize committees utilizing members of the church who are not members of the trustees in order to efficiently and effectively carry out the work of the trustees. It shall work with the treasurer and the financial secretary in the preparation and presentation of required reports regarding the financial affairs of the church. The trustee board shall make written reports to the church at regularly scheduled business meetings and at other times as may be desired.

## SECTION 4: CHRISTIAN EDUCATION/DIRECTOR

There shall be a Director of Christian Education. This individual shall be responsible for the following areas: children, youth, young adult, adult, leadership development, library, audio-visual and church training. He/She may select other members of the congregation to serve with the Director to carry out his/her responsibilities.

The Director shall be responsible for the organization, administration and supervision of the entire education program of the church. Specifically the Director shall be responsible for developing and interpreting to the constituency of the church the educational goals and objectives; studying the educational needs of the church and for making decisions concerning time schedules, educational use of equipment and facilities and the addition or elimination of classes; recruiting, training and recommending for appointment all church educational workers; determining, supervising and evaluating the curriculum of the educational program; and preparing and recommending the educational budget for the church.

The Director shall prepare a report of its activities and programs to be submitted at the regular church conference.

## ARTICLE XI
## COMMITTEES
### SECTION 1: MUSIC COMMITTEE

The Music Committee shall consist of the presidents of all choirs, and a deacon appointed by the Deacons. The Music Committee is charged with the responsibility of maintaining a quality music ministry for the church. The committee, in conjunction with the pastor, shall approve all musicians recommended for employment by the church. It shall maintain a list of all musicians in the church, in conjunction with the pastor shall select hymnals to be used for worship, provide for the proper dress of choirs, recommend instruments, oversee the maintenance of musical equipment owned by the church and recommend the music budget to the Budget Committee. The Music Committee shall designate the choir or choirs to accompany the pastor when requested. The Music Committee shall meet at least once a quarter.


## SECTION 2: BUDGET COMMITTEE

The Budget Committee shall consist of from _____ to _____ persons appointed or elected and approved by congregation. This committee shall develop and recommend an annual unified church budget. The committee shall present its recommended budget to the Deacons for review prior to submission to the membership for approval.

## SECTION 3: NOMINATING COMMITTEE

The Nominating Committee shall consist of from five (5) to nine (9) persons recommended and approved by the congregation. It shall be a representative committee and shall prepare and recommend a list of qualified candidates to fill various offices. It shall solicit input for existing boards and committee and shall ascertain the willingness of each person who is nominated to serve if elected. The committee shall present a proposed slate of officers and nominees to be voted on at the last meeting of the year. In accordance with parliamentary procedures, nominations may be made from the floor at the time the preliminary report of the committee is given.

## SECTION 4: AUDITING COMMITTEE

The church shall elect an auditing committee consisting of from _____ to _____ persons recommended by the Nominating Committee. The auditing committee shall conduct an internal audit of the financial records of the church on an annual basis. A written report shall be made at the first quarterly council meeting. Bi-annually the financial records of the church shall be audited by an external audit firm recommended by the auditing committee and approved by the church.

## SECTION 5: YOUTH DIRECTOR

The Youth Director shall be appointed by the Pastor and approved by the church. The Youth Director shall coordinate and plan activities for the youth of the church. Activities shall be designed to promote the spiritual, social and recreational development of the youth. The Youth Director shall function for the various organizations and entities within the church which plan programs for the youth.

## SECTION 6: SOCIAL COMMITTEE

The Social Committee shall be appointed by the membership to promote fellowship within the church and, when so requested by the pastor, shall be responsible for entertainment and hospitality.

## SECTION 7: COMMUNICATIONS AND PUBLICITY COMMITTEE

The Communications and Publicity Committee shall be appointed by the membership and shall make known what the church stands for and what the church has to offer programmatically. The committee shall develop and maintain a current list of all area media (newspapers, radio, t.v., etc.) and shall endeavor to promote to the broader community the activities of the church.

## SECTION 8: PULPIT COMMITTEE

See Article VII, Section 2.

## ARTICLE XII
## CHURCH OPERATIONS MANUAL

The church shall develop a church operations manual to include church policies and procedures, position descriptions, organization charts depicting lines of responsibilities in the administration of the church. The manual shall be kept in the church office and made available for use there by any member of the church. The church secretary shall maintain the manual. The manual shall be reviewed at least annually and necessary changes recommended to the church.

Addition, revision or deletion of church policies require (1) the recommendation of the church officer or organization to whose areas of assignment the policy relates; (2) approval by the church council and (3) approval by the church if the church council deems it necessary.

## ARTICLE XIII
## ELECTIONS

**SECTION 1: TIME**

The annual election of officers shall occur during the last scheduled church meeting of the year.

**SECTION 2: PROCEDURE**

At least thirty (30) days prior to the election, the Nominating Committee shall present to the church the names of one or more persons for each office to be filled. It shall be the privilege of any two (2) members, qualified to vote, to place in nomination the name of any eligible person for any office, not so nominated, and such nomination shall be placed on the ballot. No nominations shall be made from the floor at the time of the election, but each voter may vote for any one whom he or she pleases by writing in the name on the ballot. All annual elections shall be by written ballot, a majority of the ballots cast being necessary for the election of any officer. No voting by proxy shall be allowed. The church may determine any other means by which voting may be done.

## SECTION 3: TENURE OF OFFICE

The term of office for all church officers, boards and committees shall be for _____years. Church officers, boards and committee members meeting the criteria established by the church shall be eligible for re-election to additional terms.

Any church officer, board or committee member, who for a period of three (3) months, fails to faithfully perform the duties pertaining to his/her office, automatically vacates said office. Evidence of such failure to perform shall be presented to the Church Council by the Pastor. The church may, for good and sufficient cause, remove any member from office.

## SECTION 4: VACANCIES

Vacancies occurring during the year may be filled for the remainder of the unexpired term at any business meeting. The church council shall present to the church nominees for the vacancies to be filled. Elections to fill vacancies shall be by voice vote unless the church deems another procedure necessary.

## SECTION 5: ABSENTEEISM

All elected officers of the church, including auxiliary presidents, are required to attend at least seventy five (75) percent of all regular scheduled church meeting, to include regular worship services, Sunday school, Bible study and church conferences. Failure of any elected officer to attend scheduled church meetings, other than for reasons beyond his/her control, may result in the officer being removed by recommendation of the Pastor and approval by church active membership in business session.

## ARTICLE XIV

# MEETINGS
## SECTION 1: WORSHIP SERVICES

Regular public services shall be held on each Lord's Day at times fixed by the church. The Lord's Supper shall be celebrated once each month and at other times as determined by the pastor or church.

## SECTION 2: BUSINESS MEETINGS

Regularly scheduled meetings of the church and the church council shall be held every other month. The last meeting of the year shall be designated as the meeting during which time annual reports from auxiliaries shall be made, officers elected; and budget and calendar approved.

## SECTION 3: SPECIAL BUSINESS MEETINGS

Special business meetings of the church may be called by the pastor should the need arise. Notice of such meetings and the objective for which it is called shall be given on the Sunday preceding the date of the meeting. In the event that the Pastor refuses to call a special meeting, then one may also be called by petition of at least fifteen (15) percent of the active membership of the church or by a majority of the appointed or elected deacons. Notice and purpose for which it is called will be given at least one week in advance.

## SECTION 4: QUORUM

A quorum necessary for the transaction of business other than the election or dismissal of a pastor shall consist of fifteen (15) qualified voters. A quorum shall consist of twenty (20%) percent of the active membership of the church for the purpose of a call or dismissal of a pastor.

Only members in good standing shall have the right to vote on business matters and for the call or dismissal of a pastor. (Give criteria for a member in good standing).

For reasons beyond one's circumstances, such as sickness, employment, age, etc., one may be a member in good standing for good cause shown; provided, a majority of the members present deem that good cause has been shown.

## ARTICLE XV
## CHURCH YEAR
The fiscal year of the church shall commence on the 1 day of January and end on the 3 1 day of December.

## ARTICLE XVI
## RULES OF ORDER
These Constitution and By-laws, Holy Scriptures and Hiscox Directory shall be the guide for the church and the rules contained in Robert's Rules of Order shall govern the business proceedings of this church in all cases.

## ARTICLE XVII
## AMENDMENTS
This Constitution may be amended at any regular or called business meeting of the church provided the recommended amendments have been submitted in writing at a previous business meeting. Approval of amendments requires a two-thirds (2/3) vote of those present provided a quorum has been met.

## ARTICLE XVIII
## RATIFICATION
The Constitution and By-laws shall become effective immediately after approval by the church.

APPROVED AND ADOPTED BY (NAME CHURCH) AT A SPECIAL CALL MEETING HELD ON _____.

This the _____ day of _____, _____.

_____Pastor

_____Church Clerk

## Sample Pastor and Church Agreement

**THIS AGREEMENT** is made between
_____(church) located at (address) and
_____(pastor) located at (address).

**WHEREAS,** Pastor is a minister of the gospel and is qualified to serve as pastor of this church.

**WHEREAS,** Church is in need of a pastor to minister to the congregation and to oversee the administration of the church

**WHEREAS,** The membership of this church has duly considered the application of Pastor to serve as pastor of this church and pastor can contribute to the success of this church's spiritual, financial and secular needs.

**WHEREAS,** Church and pastor desire to enter into a contract for the employment of pastor on the terms and conditions set forth,

**NOW THEREFORE** in consideration of the mutual covenants, conditions and promises contained in this agreement, it is agreed as follows

1. **Employment and duties:** Church hereby employs pastor and pastor hereby accepts and agrees to such employment. The pastor's duties and responsibilities are as follows:
(Set out the duties and responsibilities)

2. **Term of employment agreement:**
(Set out the terms of the agreement)

3. **Compensation:**
   a. Salary (Set salary and terms)
   b. Housing allowance

4. **Benefits:** The pastor will also receive the following benefits during his agreement.

(List Benefits)

5. **Expenses:** Church will agree to reimburse pastor for any reasonable out-of pocket expense he/she advances in the performances of his/her services prescribed herein.

6. **Representation and warranties:** Pastor warrants and represents the following

A. Pastor is a minister of the gospel and is ordained by the _____(church) or _____(association).

B Pastor is an experienced pastor and will abide by the policies and procedures established by the church.

C. Pastor will attend all regularly scheduled church meetings and other official functions of the church unless illness or other emergencies make attendance impossible.

7. Pastor agrees not to be employed or engaged in activities substantially similar to those covered by this agreement without church prior consent.

8. **Termination:**
(Set out grounds for termination)

9. (Set out any other matters of agreement)

**IN WITNESS WHEREOF**, the parties have executed this agreement as of the date listed below.

_____Church

By_____

_____Pastor

# Bibliography

Beecher, Henry Ward. *Famous Quotes*

McCaleb, George. *Faithful Over A Few Things.* Orman Press, 2000

Odle, Joe T. *Church Member's Handbook.* B & H Publishing Group, 1986

Mott, Stephen Charles. *Biblical Ethics and Social Change.* Oxford University Press, 1982

Power, Bruce P. *Church Administration.* Broadman Press, Nashville, Tennessee, 1985

Schwertley, Brian. *Conflict Resolution In The Church.* eHow Culture & Society

Smith, J. Alfred. *Deacons Upholding The Pastor's Arms.* Progressive National Baptist Publishing House, 1983

Tidwell, Charles A. *Church Administration, Effective Leadership For Ministry.* Broadman Press, Nashville, Tennessee, 1985

Warren, Rick. *The Purpose Driven Church.* Zondervan Publishing House, Grand Rapids, Michigan, 1995

18965724R00056

Made in the USA
Charleston, SC
30 April 2013